THE
NAKED I

THE
NAKED I

seeking God and finding identity

Eileen Guder

word books, publisher, waco, texas

Contents

1. The First Question — 7
2. The Search Goes On — 17
3. False Meanings — 26
4. The Unwanted Self — 38
5. Identity Given by God — 50
6. A Case of Mistaken Identity — 59
7. But Don't Change Me! — 69
8. The Eye of the Needle — 76
9. The Double Face of Change — 85
10. Identity in Relationships — 97
11. Identity in Function — 109
12. Filling the Role — 118
13. The Limits of the Role — 126
14. God's Originals — 134

1. The First Question

$W_{hat\ your\ generation}$ doesn't understand," the young man said to me, "is that we're looking for reality. We're not going to settle for just a job and a wife and family. We want more than a split-level home in suburbia, an executive's salary and retirement benefits. We're looking for the meaning of life."

It might have been me, or any one of my generation, saying those words. My young friend, who had us neatly filed and mentally labeled, would have had difficulty accepting that, but it was true. For all the scowling intensity of his eyes, holding mine as if by the force of his gaze he could make me understand, Harry never really saw me. He saw *his image* of me. Not only that, he never heard me. He kept talking about his honesty, his hatred of phoniness, his contempt for materialism, his willingness to be vulnerable.

"I do know how you feel," I interrupted at one

point, "because I have felt just the same way. I wanted to be a real person, to do something worthwhile in the world . . ."

"Your ideas of what was worthwhile are part of our problem," he burst in. Then he went on to tell me what I and all my generation thought, hoped, feared, and worked for, just as if he could read our minds. Everything he said was a caricature.

For a moment I was furious at the arrogance of Harry's words. He was talking about reality and honesty, but he wasn't seeing reality or even being honest. He was viewing the world through a distorted lens, seeing people not as they were, but as he supposed them to be.

But then I recalled my own youthful brashness, my own conviction that the older generation had never thought the profound thoughts *I* was thinking, had never been seized by the same passionate hunger for reality. I had been guilty of the same dishonesty and distortion.

The phrase "your generation" uttered accusingly has been around a long time. When had I stopped using it (even mentally) to my parents? The past has a way of telescoping, and complex events are remembered in bold outlines, so I don't recall how long it took for my viewpoint to change. In retrospect, however, I realized that my ability to see my father and mother as three-dimensional people was somehow connected with the conviction that I had, at last, come face to face with reality.

After Harry left, I sat for a long time, remembering.

There are some memories that remain in all their color and clarity unblurred by time. In an instant, between breaths or without pausing in our conversation, the past is sharp and clear for a moment. One such fragment out of my past comes to me frequently. I can see now, in my mind's eye, the view of my neighborhood spread below me as I sat on a hillside above. I was fourteen. We lived on the last street up the hill. There were a few houses across the street, and beyond them the foothills, rising gently above the town.

On that summer day I had hiked alone looking for wildflowers—Indian paintbrush, lupin, mariposa lilies. A brisk wind was blowing and I sat, the flowers I had picked beside me, looking over the rooftops below to the Pacific Ocean beyond. To my left there was a gully and then another gently rounded hill. As I watched it seemed to be covered with delicate green water—running uphill. I knew it was only the wild grasses blown by the wind, but the illusion was so strong it almost had a reality of its own.

I remember thinking long, chaotic thoughts about the nature of reality. What was I seeing? Was it only grass blowing in the wind, transformed for a moment into running water? Did reality lie in what it was—or in what I saw? What was really beyond and behind the visible world of earth and trees and all the innumerable works of man, all the houses and furniture and machinery and objects that have been made out of our world and its fecundity? Where would I find the meaning of it all?

In a few years I began to realize that this same

longing for reality was the undertone to every human relationship I knew. The yearning we all feel for some glimpse of truth, for a rationale behind the bewildering perplexity of the universe, is the other side of our hunger for human companionship. We want reality. But reality consists of the *meaning* of the universe and human existence. All the scientific knowledge possible, though it tells us what things are and what they are made of, doesn't tell us why they are.

We can look forever at the stars through increasingly powerful telescopes and never find significance to life. When it comes to significance, we turn not to the physical world around us but to each other. Meaning is found only in relationships, and our relationships are predicated on the assumption that response is possible.

The longing to be responded to is very deep. I don't believe it can be analyzed. Like love and fear and all of life's basic drives, it is "just there." But it is very strong and is perhaps the reason why we have from time immemorial invested the physical world with personality. Trees are more than wood, sap, and leaves —they are dryads. Rivers and oceans and mountains are personified as spirits, beings capable of response.

We want more than just an intellectual knowledge of reality; we want to *know* in the sense of communicating with. And we want to be known. We want to be known as we really are and to know others the same way. That ought to be simple, but very early in life we all learn it is not. We have become small bundles of contradictions which make all our ties with other people very complicated.

We long to be known—but we are afraid to be known. There are so many traits in each of us which we don't like and which we conceal as effectively as we can. We want to know others truly, not merely to exchange pleasantries. But some people seem threatening to us, so we wall them off in a handy category rather than risk being hurt. Most of all, we want to be accepted and we fear rejection. As many others have done, I often found it easier to reject as a protective device: do it to others before they do it to you.

That was one way of protecting myself from being hurt. I learned it very early, along with another useful device—discover what kind of performance will best disarm the people who might possibly cut through to some vulnerable spot, and then play it to the hilt. All my timidity and uncertainty could, I found, be effectively concealed if I amused my contemporaries, so I became a clown. I was a duffer at games, but if I overplayed my clumsiness and made a joke of myself, I was laughed at but not derided. That was my way of hiding the real me who might be dreadfully wounded if she came out in the open. There are lots of other ways of hiding—being the best student (I worked hard at that too) or the prettiest girl or the most popular or even the most self-assured.

All these methods are still being used. A friend of mine was telling me one day about her conversation with two high school girls. They were leaders in their group and so self-assured and competent, so arrogant in their careless snubbing of others, that my friend, an advisor to the group, took them to lunch to discuss the problem.

The talk went slowly. The girls were disdainful and even a little amused as the advisor fumbled for a gracious way to tell them they had been unkind and snobbish. In the end she spoke frankly and their composure cracked. As she continued, trying to be constructive, she said finally, "Look, girls, you don't have to put up this phony front in order to be leaders—just be yourselves!"

At that one girl broke into tears and sobbed, "But then nobody would like me!"

There is our dilemma. The very truth we must find if we are to know what life is all about may be not only a glimpse of the Reality behind the universe but an unretouched picture of ourselves. And that we will not allow; we must hide that picture away—from ourselves, but especially from wives and husbands and children and friends. We can so easily imagine their disappointment, even their dislike if they knew what we were really like.

My own personal search for meaning was complicated by the hidden fear that in my looking I might stumble upon my real self and find it intolerable. Thinking about myself was an uncomfortable business because there were so many layers of protective wrappings—the clown, the A-student, the self-sufficient loner who never spoke to anyone who might reject her. I wasn't sure the real me (if there was one) could ever be found. But oh, if there were someone who did know me as I really was and who loved and accepted me without reservation, perhaps I might be of some worth.

I've been sitting here for a long time trying to find some words to help me describe the experience which convinced me I was known and loved—and there aren't any. That's the way with the most real happenings in our lives, the events that take place in our thinking and feeling. They are real but indescribable. We have to use similes, or metaphors, or strings of adjectives in an attempt to communicate the untellable, and we never quite succeed. How do you convey to another person what it's like to be in love, or frozen with fear, or fragmented by grief? Or how it is that one can sit in an ordinary room on an ordinary chair and *know* suddenly that God is real and that he cares? That's what happened to me during those adolescent years, and the experience was genuine enough to have not only lasted but deepened.

Sitting in the living room one day I thought, *What if there isn't a God at all? What if there's nothing, nobody, to make sense out of life? What will happen to me?*

I was so frightened at this glimpse of emptiness that I began to pray. "O God, if you're out there, anywhere, I *have to know*—please, please, let me know if you're there."

And God did. I can't tell you how or why I'm so sure it was real—only that I knew, suddenly, that he was there, that I wasn't alone, and that he knew all about me and loved me. It was the first touch of the reality I was looking for. I knew also that God had done something concrete about me in Jesus' life and teaching, and supremely in his death, which I accepted

13 / The First Question

without in the least understanding any of its implications. God also began to show me something else—myself.

Most of my Christian life, it seems to me, has been spent in unwinding myself from the cocoon of delusions, excuses, self-deceits, and fears in which I had been hiding. I am still at it. Like those two high school girls I was (and sometimes still am) secretly afraid no one would like me as I know myself to be. God might—but people wouldn't. I know my own readiness to judge others. Can I expect more from them than I have been able to give? How safe *is* life as a Christian? How honest can I be without getting hurt? Sincerity, while always highly praised, is risky.

Perhaps one reason sincerity is such an admired virtue is that all of us know how rare it is. In our most candid moments we know that despite our efforts to be without pretense we are not capable of total transparency. How could we be? We do not even understand our own motives nor the tortuous workings of our own minds. We do the best we can but we are still people who "see as in a glass, darkly."

Yet we cannot escape the desire for honesty and truth in personal relationships, nor its other side, the longing for reality and meaning to life. Most religions have placed an emphasis on some standard of behavior which is thought to conform to objective truth. We don't think it through—we just know that if there is truth in the universe then truth is demanded of us as human beings.

Knowing what we ought to be is one thing, however.

Living up to it is another. From earliest times we have demonstrated our knowledge of our inability to be what we should be in the elaborate systems of ritual, sacrifice, and penance contained in our religions. Outside of religion, there are other, subtler ways of handling the terrifying consciousness that we are not "up to" the demands of God—rationalizations, busyness, burying oneself in any number of things. All of us are caught in the same predicament—longing to know, fearing to be known.

The way out of the predicament has gradually become clear. The reality I had been looking for all my life I found in God. But not really in knowing him—after all, my knowledge of the supreme Fact of the universe is infinitesimal. My security lies in the realization that he knows *me*. The terror of being known and rejected began to vanish as I realized that I was known—and accepted.

I also began to learn the implications of Jesus Christ's life and death. I began to learn that I needed to be rescued from my own inability to live a good life. There had been enough "sins" in my short history for me to comprehend that beneath them lay sin, a disease of the soul, and I accepted Christ's capability of dealing with that. Those little sins—piddling and unimportant as they were—yet might grow to gigantic and horrendous proportions, and as often as not were committed in order to protect the image I had created of myself.

Christ came, I began to see, not just to save us from the despair and guilt of sin, but from our delusions. We are not just to know the truth, or as much of it as we are able to understand; we are to *become* the truth. Sin is not doing bad things. It is being warped persons, bound to conceptions and ideas of ourselves and our world that lead to greedy, lustful, arrogant acts. I found the answer to my question, "Is there meaning and reality to be found?" in accepting Christ. It also meant accepting his truth and being committed to reality.

Life is a process of discarding the illusions we have wrapped about us. We have all used myths to shield ourselves from the chill knowledge of our own inadequacy. That is all very well for the skeptic. He needs something to keep out the cold, to ward off the terror of cosmic night. But when one has met Christ and recognized him as the ultimate reality who has come to be with us and to turn our unreality into truth, myths and fables must go.

That is what this book is all about—adventures and discoveries on the journey from the false to the real, from shadow to substance. It's about what happens as we come out from behind the illusion and show the real self—the naked I.

2. The Search Goes On

*T*rying *to find* a meaning to life isn't something we do only when we sit down and think, "Now, I'm going to concentrate on discovering some meaning to life." We are working at it all the time.

Each day we are engaged in living on two levels. On one level are the events taking place which in some way involve us. The other is what we are thinking about the events—our reactions to them. Every time we talk with someone we are evaluating and reacting not just to the words spoken, but to the attitude, the tone of voice, the general impression the other person is making. And there is always the possibility that we may read into his words meaning he never meant to convey.

I remember well how, as a child, hearing a certain strident note in my father's voice I began to shiver inside with nervousness and fear. That angry tone was usually the forerunner of a sound spanking. Today a similar tone of voice produces the same involuntary fear, a state of response I have learned to dislike exceedingly; entirely irrational, of course. The speaker may be merely very much in earnest, not angry at all. But it is always an effort for me to put down the negative feelings of my purely instinctive reaction and listen for the *real* message.

The meanings we attribute to the attitudes around us are not always so negative, of course. Women are quite often justly accused of building a fantasy world out of nothing more than a courteous sentence—when we want to believe the words meant more than they said. I've done it myself, countless times, and felt like a fool afterwards, which helps me understand the younger women who come to me with long, involved stories leading nowhere. How many times have I heard detailed accounts of conversations in which the most matter-of-fact statements are invested (by the eager girl) with emotional content that simply wasn't there.

Some years ago a young friend of mine fancied herself in love with her employer, a handsome and personable man of about thirty-five. She was fairly inexperienced as a typist and file clerk, and was the recipient of much patient correction and tactful hints meant to help her be an efficient worker. All of these, when they came from her boss, were seen by my imaginative friend as indications of romantic interest on his part. My carefully casual questions about the nature of his suggestions, all of which pertained strictly to business, were airily dismissed. About the time she was certain he would ask her for a date, he fired her —kindly, tactfully, but firmly—as just not competent for the job she had been hired for.

Even our casual impressions of those around us can be so colored. The ideas we come away with—he was angry, she was irritated, he likes me, she dislikes me —may be very wide of the mark. They may be erroneous impressions, and for a number of reasons. Fatigue, fear, shyness, dislike, or wishful thinking—all these things are delicately shading our impressions of the world and people around, and the shading may distort or obscure the reality.

Just as we live life on two levels, every event takes place on two levels—what actually is happening, and what people *think* is happening. How difficult, then, for any of us to see things as they really are! And if we did, what would we have? Nothing but a list of facts about attitudes, events, conversations, and behavior. We would still be obliged to find some meaning to explain those facts. For that which is real, genuine, objective in its existence—not a myth, not an illusion, *just there*—presents us, by reason of its existence, with many questions. A mountain, a smile, a tree, a rock, a sudden shout of anger, a blow, a deformed child, a symphony—what do they tell us about life unless we find the answers to the questions they pose? Why is it there? What is it for? Who put it there? What will it be in the future?

While these questions were rumbling about in my thinking in a most uncomfortable way (for such queries must make us uncomfortable, otherwise we would never bother to find answers), I was aware that there were two approaches to the problem of meaning. I had used only one.

That way had been to try to figure out what was behind every single episode in my life as it came along. I must weigh and measure, evaluate motives and the sincerity of persons, look for hidden objectives, and hope that as time went on some sort of pattern would emerge. This pattern, hopefully, would give me a clue to the grand design of life—or the universe—or whatever phrase you choose to describe the question, "What's it all about?"

On the other hand, I could give up the attempt to understand everything as it happened and look for the answer to the ultimate question, "Is there any reality or meaning to life at all? And if so, in what does it lie?" Eventually I had to come to the second way, not because I thought it all out and judiciously decided that was best, but because I came to see Jesus Christ as *the* center and source of all meaning. And also, if I must be truthful, because I was making such a botch of life using the first method.

Jesus Christ assured us that God loves us, and he himself demonstrated the Father's love and concern, because he and the Father are one. He offered the answer to the question, "Is there meaning to life?" The answer was "Yes," because God was there, bringing order and beauty to what seemed chaos. The confusion, and seemingly meaningless torrent of events which make up history were because of man's sin, not because there had been no order planned. I could accept that, because I realized how much disorder and confusion my own wrong thinking had contributed to my life, and to the lives of those around me. I had added my own bit of meaninglessness to history.

Again and again I found that I had misunderstood, misinterpreted, and wrongly judged people's attitudes, what they said, and what they did. I was wrong more than I was right. And the wrongness of my deductions was, I saw, largely the result of problems within myself. My own insecurities, resentments, malice, and envy were the ground out of which I was producing such a bitter crop of presuppositions and errors.

In telling about my own search for meaning to life, I do not want to give the impression that, having become a Christian, I sat down and thought it all out. What can be compressed into a few pages took place over a number of years, with long periods when I put the whole issue by and gave myself to the urgencies of life growing up, getting married, and being a wife and the mother of three children.

The passion for reality which I had felt when I first accepted Christ as an adolescent girl faded sometimes to a faint whisper. Underneath all the busyness and worries and small cares of life it was there, however, and it had a way of popping up with awkward questions. "Do you really want to settle for this?" "Are you sure you'll be happy now?" "Is this *all* you want out of life?" "Is Christ satisfied with you?" It was loudest of all when my efforts to build a nice, tidy, untroubled life for myself met with frustration.

When I entered marriage I had the hope that perhaps now I would find fulfillment and could end my search. In spite of all the poets and song writers, however, love—that is, love between men and women—isn't all there is to life. I found that it left all the ultimate questions unanswered.

Children add a marvelous new dimension, but they are themselves, not an extension of one's own ego. They bring new problems and new questions with them, but they certainly bring no answers. I was discovering that it isn't possible to throw oneself into anything—marriage, motherhood, even church work or philanthropy—and suddenly find all life's questions answered. It is possible, for women of a certain temperament, to plunge into a cause or a relationship with such vehemence that there is no time left to consider anything but the moment's demands. But that is no answer; it is merely a postponement of the inevitable recurring question.

If I had expected that becoming a Christian would give me "inside information" about the difficult questions of life, I soon saw it did not. Apparently Jesus never meant his followers to have that kind of advantage. We were not to be like people who have influential friends in the government who pass on tips about pending legislative action, or executive decrees. We were in the world just like everybody else, with no special favors given.

There didn't seem to be any hidden or esoteric keys to the perplexities of life in the New Testament, either. The more I read, the only thing I saw clearly was its words about what my attitudes should be, how I ought to live, and what Jesus expected of me. Even the words in the fourteenth chapter of John which I had so often read as a sort of blanket promise by God to take care of me were not quite what I had thought. Jesus *did* say, "Whatever you ask in my name, I will do it that the Father may be glorified in the Son: if you ask anything in my name, I will do it" (John 14:13, 14, RSV).

How comforting! But a closer reading took away some of the comfort and added a stringent demand upon *me*. Jesus had been talking about his oneness with the Father, doing God's work just as the disciples were to do. He followed his promise to grant them whatever they asked in his name by a description of the people who are his, the ones who can make requests of him. These people know his commandments and obey them. They are like branches of a vine, letting the life of the vine flow through them to produce fruit. They have the kind of love for each other that Christ has—to the point of dying for them if necessary. They will be hated by those who hate Christ, and will be persecuted. They may even be killed by people who think that is what God wants. They will have joy, Christ's joy—but that is not incompatible with a great deal of distress, because Jesus concluded the whole passage by saying, "You will find trouble in the world —but, never lose heart, I have conquered the world!"

There it was. The last night Jesus had with the few men who would carry on his work in the world, and all he told them about what he was doing was that it would cause them trouble! No timetable laid out before them, no explanation of human suffering, or why there are wars, or what will happen to those who have never heard of Jesus—not one glimpse, in fact, of the inner workings of God's kingdom. Nothing but instructions on how we are to live, and a warning that living that way won't be easy.

It seems, then, that just as we find meaning to life in Christ we are supposed to go on finding it in him, not in being let into God's secrets. I began to see that my whole attention ought to be given to living, as much as I can, the way Christ wants me to, not in figuring out what he intends to do, or how he'll work this or that out.

That doesn't mean that we're not to do all we can to explore the wonders of our universe, and to understand each other better. God gave us curious minds for a purpose, and a whole world to use them in. It *does* mean that we will never know enough to wrap up all the mysteries of life in tidy little explanations. We will always have to say, "With the information we have at hand, it seems . . . ," realizing that he hasn't told us everything, only enough to live by.

Many years after I first began to think about the meaning to life, I came across a passage in Ephesians which fairly jumped out of the page. I'd slid easily and lightly over it before, but here it was, the reply to my question, "Is there meaning to life?" written about A.D. 62 for circulation to some churches in Asia:

For God has allowed us to know the secret of his plan, and it is this: he purposes in his sovereign will that all human history shall be consummated in Christ, that everything that exists in Heaven or earth shall find its perfection and fulfillment in him.

It fitted in with what I knew already—that the ultimate question is answered, but we have to work out the little ones as we go along. That's what I'm doing every day. "What does it mean to be a Christian wife—mother—friend—businessman—student—in this world, this present situation?" Questions like this must be dealt with, not by abstract reasoning, but by the way we live.

It's all very different than I imagined it would be when I was a pudgy adolescent, dreaming about my future. I thought growing up and becoming mature meant *knowing* a great deal. I find instead it means *being* what God meant me to be. The way is not by penetrating secret places of knowledge, but by doing what I already know to be right.

It may be that God is always nudging us back into reality. We like to dream, to let our thoughts drift into the shadowy unknown, the cloudy realm of speculation and hypothesis. "What if . . . do you suppose . . . can it be?" we say, hoping to discover some hitherto veiled secret which will make all mysteries known. But Jesus says to us, "Happy are the humble-minded—the merciful—the sincere . . . love your enemies . . . forgive other people their failures . . . don't pile up treasures on earth . . . don't criticize people . . ." plain, practical words about living ordinary lives and getting along with people.

25 / *The Search Goes On*

3. False
Meanings

Some years ago a national magazine ran a series of articles by various people prominent in their profession. The subject was the meaning of life. There were as many explanations of the meaning of life as there were articles, but they had one common element. Each writer found the meaning of life—and a rationale for the universe—in terms of his own discipline. The geneticist explained everything in terms of genetics, the biologist within the framework of biology, the economist according to his understanding of economics.

They had one further element in common; they all drew conclusions from their particular science about how men ought to behave. They agreed that man ought to be good—that is, kind, considerate, honest, careful of the rights of others, and so on. They disagreed on the reason *why* he ought to be so and why, in spite of his best efforts, he failed so frequently.

On reading these articles I was struck very forcibly by the evidence of our incurable tendency to look for pattern in the universe. Few of the writers mentioned any orthodox religion, but they all drew religious conclusions from their study; they imposed a pattern of behavior which, in some sense, they justified on the grounds of the pattern they had observed in their area of study.

It does not seem logical to me to look for the rationale, the meaning, of the whole universe in a study devoted to a small part of it, such as one science. True, some sciences can tell you what has happened in the universe, or what is now happening. But they can never tell why, nor to what end. Any explanation of the mystery of the universe and the life we live ought to come from something bigger than the whole, not from a part of it.

Still, it's very human to generalize, which is what the writers of these articles were doing. It is what we do when we say, "All Frenchmen are . . . ," or "Men are always . . . ," or (as small children do when they are balked), "I *never* get to have any fun!"

Some of the best advertising slogans are generalizations. The idea, for instance, beloved by cosmetic firms, that blondes have more fun; or that getting rid of bad breath makes a girl popular and lovable. Deciding, on the basis of one unhappy love affair, that all women are faithless is not the same as applying the observable workings of one area of life to the entire universe, yet it's all the same kind of reasoning. From knowledge or experience of one instance or one segment of life we draw conclusions about the whole.

Of course, this innate tendency man has toward discovering patterns in the world is a very necessary thing. Without it we would never learn anything about our world. We'd always be surprised that water flows downhill and the sun rises in the east. Knowledge comes because we are creatures who have an urge to categorize, systematize, theorize. The problem, as far as finding ultimate answers is concerned, is that when we look for answers to our questions about the meaning of life in studies of its parts, we are looking in the wrong place. There is nothing at all in our physical world which tells us what it's all about. Paul's remarks in the first chapter of Romans that the world shows enough of God's attributes to make idolatry a sin do not mean that God can be *known* through nature. We can know something about him—that he is immensely powerful and that he created order and pattern. But that tells us nothing of his purpose or his intentions toward us, or of any possible goal to life.

For that we needed some other gesture from God— exactly what he did in revealing himself personally, first to individuals like Noah, Abraham, and Moses, then in his mighty acts in behalf of a small tribal nation, and finally and ultimately in the Incarnation. God's revelation was ultimate as far as this life is concerned. We are told there will be more in the next: "We only know that, if reality were to break through, we should reflect his likeness, for we should see him as he really is!"

The Naked I / 28

What God did, as a matter of fact, was to reveal himself in an intensely personal way to individual persons. We are wrong, therefore, when we expect science or any part of it to tell us anything about God. All it does is observe his world.

But scientists are men with all the usual human failings, and when a scientist rejects—or hasn't heard—the revelation God has given of himself, he does pretty much what people have always done—imposes some rationale on the universe because we cannot stand to live in a world without pattern.

As Christians we have a different situation. We have been shown the meaning of life and the goal toward which all history moves. Paul put it in the words I quoted in the last chapter: God "purposes in his sovereign will that all human history shall be consummated in Christ, that everything that exists in Heaven or earth shall find its perfection and fulfillment in him." We've seen the total picture, the mystery has been unveiled, and we are, so to speak, "in the know" about the ultimate end of life.

But—and this is a very large caution—we can easily make the same mistake in reasoning as the person bent on explaining everything in terms of his science. We do it in reverse. We like to think that not only do we know the purpose of God in the world and what he wants in our lives, but that all the detailed workings of the world have been explained to us. We are always passing judgment on scientific truth not on the basis of its demonstrability but on the Bible. We make the Bible say things about science as if it were a textbook of all human knowledge instead of God's word about himself in relationship to us.

The church has always suffered in the end when she confused scientific truth with revealed truth about God in history. Galileo was the victim of this kind of thinking—for a time. But truth, like murder, will out and in the end the church had to face the fact that her view of God's world was too small to fit the facts.

Even if we don't make that particular mistake, if we are willing to let men's increasing knowledge of our world expand, as I believe God meant it to, we are often still busy trying to figure out what he's up to. We think because he's told us enough for salvation, enough to live according to his will (and who has ever succeeded in doing all we've been told?), that there won't be any ambiguities in life. We sometimes treat God like a chef doing a demonstration on television, explaining just what he's doing and why. We want everything dissected, categorized, and summarized so that there are no mysteries left in life. Do dogs and cats go to heaven? There must be a verse in the Bible about that. Are there rational beings on other planets? Chapter and verse are hunted for the answer. Some of the matters supposedly dealt with are trivial, others are far more serious.

What about the heathen who never had a chance to hear the gospel? Be careful before you answer that question by consigning them all to hell. Paul, who was shown secrets you and I do not know, wrote to the Romans: "When Gentiles who have not the law do by nature what the law requires, *they are a law to them-*

selves, even though they do not have the law. They show that what the law requires is written on their hearts, while their conscience also bears witness and their conflicting thoughts accuse or perhaps excuse them on that day when, according to my gospel, God judges the secrets of men by Christ Jesus" (Romans 2:14-16, RSV, my italics).

We know that the way to come to God the Father is through Jesus Christ—but God hasn't told us all the resources at his command. Or anything at all about the plight of the man who hasn't had a chance to hear, other than Paul's words and Jesus' very sobering and puzzling parable of the sheep and the goats in Matthew 25. In short, we just don't know everything. It is arrogant conceit to assume that we can speak with divine authority on all questions.

Nor does the Christian faith serve as a handy encyclopedia one can refer to when puzzled by mysteries of behavior, or the oddities of nature. The Bible won't tell us secrets science may discover, nor make psychology an unnecessary study. Both science and psychology, however, are fields of inquiry into what we might call the technicalities of life. Why does such-and-such happen in the natural world, and why does old so-and-so behave the way he does? Those are questions for science or psychology. Other questions must be answered by other disciplines. But all the answers in the world about these matters will never reveal the central mystery—is there meaning to life? And if there is, where do we find it? We have the ultimate answer in Christ; isn't that enough?

One woman used to spend hours studying various authorities so she could prove to her Sunday school class that evolution as a theory was all wrong and that the Bible told us all we need to know about the origin of human life. She was obsessed with the need to find an answer to every question about the development of man in Scripture. To this end obscure passages of the Old Testament were analyzed and dissected, and elaborate explanations built around them. Great care was taken to examine every word of certain books of the Bible in the hope that the mysteries of the past would be made plain. While she was doing all this her only daughter was gradually drifting away from faith in Christ, turned off by her mother's insensitivity toward her as a person and disgusted with what she saw to be an unhealthy preoccupation with the past. Her mother had forgotten, if she ever knew, that the Bible is a book about relationships, not about categories of knowledge.

Moses reminded the ancient Jews of our human limitations when he said, "The secret things belong to the Lord our God; but the things that are revealed belong to us and to our children forever, that we may do all the words of this law" (Deut. 29:29, RSV).

There is the clue to what we've been told—and what we haven't. We have been told *enough to do* "all the words of this law." And judging by human performance, we've been told more than enough. We rarely succeed in doing what we know to be right. It seems to me that a very horrifying transference takes place when we insist on being authorities on everything. We neglect the plain teachings of the Bible in favor of the obscure, the hidden, the secret things God has kept for himself; and we fail to do what we ought to do.

We are wrong when we attempt to explain everything that takes place, as if knowing our final destiny insured our also understanding the intricacies and complexities of men and stars. There has to be a "reason" for everything, and the reason has to be obvious. This makes God into a cosmic stage director, busy sending people on and off at the right times and shifting the scenery.

A friend once said to me, "Now I wonder why I had to go to the hospital. God must have had someone there for me to meet." The primary reason she had to go to the hospital, I felt sure, was that she was ill. And I do *not* believe that God made her ill just so she could go to the hospital, like a playwright maneuvering his characters together in a scene. Don't misunderstand me. I believe that everything that happens to us—all the episodes of each day and all we ourselves say and do—fits into God's providence. There is nothing we can do, nothing we can undergo, that is outside his love and concern and knowledge. But *everything* includes all the wrong things we do, either because of deliberately choosing to do so or because we have limited or misleading information to act on, as well as all the wrongs done to us, and the natural forces of our physical life. God does not *make* us do anything.

I do not know why certain events fall out as they do, why good people suffer unjustly at times, or why death and disease strike certain ones and not others.

In a general way, of course, I know that sin and suffering are part of this world's evil, which Christ came to do away with; that the pain and distress we go through here will be as nothing in eternity. In short, I know enough of God's love and concern to trust him for the big questions. But the details are shrouded in God's inscrutability.

That's good—better than knowing all the answers (or thinking one knows them) to the minutiae of life but unable to see the big picture. The substance of my faith *is* the big picture—God's purpose for the world and for me. It doesn't matter to me that I don't understand all the small events that are part of the big picture; after all, God is painting on an immense canvas, and each of us sees only a minute bit of it. To expect that we should immediately be able to say of everything in life, "Yes, of course, this is the way it is because . . ." is spiritual arrogance.

How God is able to bring eventual good out of the obvious evil in the world we cannot understand, other than simply accepting the fact that eternity waits for us all, and that we have been promised that there things will be as they ought to be.

That leaves us free to abandon the attempt to see how God is working things out in every situation. He *does not* move us about like pawns on a chessboard, nor arrange situations conveniently around us in order to teach us something or to answer our prayers. *How* our prayers are answered, and how the seeming confusion of this life is resolved into his order remains, as it ought to, his secret.

I finally gave up the attempt to figure out how God was working in the world. The reasons I have just discussed were partly responsible. I didn't think all this through overnight. It took years of blundering about, tacking interpretations onto circumstances and people which usually turned out to be demonstrably false. Every time this happened I was reminded of all the bad guesses I had made about the attitudes and motives of others, based on *my* impressions, or how the tone of voice struck me. It occurred to me that I had wasted a lot of time in fruitless speculations. I began to think about the catchword often used as a greeting, "What do you know for sure?"

The one sure thing we do know about this life is that we won't lead trouble-free lives. Jesus pointed that out to his disciples again and again, remarking one time that "the servant is not greater than his master." We can all speak knowledgeably about the meaning of events in his life, how he fulfilled Old Testament prophecies, and accomplished the purpose of his Father. But was it plain then?

Since Jesus was a true man, not just deity in disguise, so to speak, his life was not in any sense like a walk-through part. Faith and commitment and obedience were required of him, too. We are reminded in the book to the Hebrew Christians that Jesus is the leader of our salvation, made perfect through the fact that he suffered and was tempted just as we are tempted. One of the standard temptations we all are faced with is the temptation to conclude that life is meaningless. Christians, too, are tempted to succumb to that at times. Some pain and some suffering we can accept, especially if we feel we deserve punishment, or must learn a lesson. But when trouble goes on and on, and there's no "reason" for it, then the temptation to despair becomes very strong. Surely Jesus felt that temptation and conquered it.

The secret of facing trouble with serenity lies in our conviction of ultimate good, ultimate right,—*not* in being able to figure out why things happen as they do. The purpose of God includes all my thinking and doing, as all of yours, and everything that both good and bad men are up to.

To say that he *uses* the evil that men do—such as Pharaoh's decision not to let the Israelites go—is not the same as saying that he *makes* men do evil. We will be tempted to explore that path, to speculate on the difference between his perfect will and his permissive will, to moralize about the lessons he may teach us. But we'd be better off to refrain. Leave the secrets to him.

As I write this, a friend of many years' standing is ill with an incurable ailment. Her unquenchable optimism has nothing to do with what is happening to her body; it is based on her relationship to Christ. She doesn't have to have the answers to questions like, "Why has this happened to me?" and, "How can this illness be part of the plan of a good and loving God?" She *knows* God. The answers can wait.

In the years I've known her we've done a lot of talking about ourselves, about life and our relationship to Christ and how we live because of it. But now that I come to think of it, all she has meant and does mean to me and all the help she has been as a friend is not because she could answer whatever questions troubled me, but because of what she is as a person. That's what the Bible is for—to help us become what we are capable of as Christ's men and women, not to make us walking encyclopedias.

4. The Unwanted Self

All I know about myself I know in, and because of, relationships. That's why I can't get too excited, as I indicated in the last chapter, about finding out all sorts of hidden clues to what makes the world tick. The most important matters are "Who am I? Am I worthwhile?" and "Who are *you*—can we know each other?"

These are still the most vital questions in life. Like me, and like many others, today's young adults are trying to find answers to the same questions, although their methods of seeking may differ from ours. Today even more than before, this is an especially acute issue because many of the old ways in which people found identity are gone. Family identity, tribal identity, community identity, even national identity, have thinned so as to be nearly transparent. Our sons and daughters, growing up in an affluent society and in a world where communication brings us almost instant knowledge of events everywhere, are shouting the questions we whispered under our breath. They want to know who they are—as well as to find meaning in life.

I wanted to know that, too, but because the state of the world was far different from what it is now, I, like others of my generation, had to face more immediate issues. We had to find jobs and to hold them in a depression-ridden society. The longing to know one's own identity was there, but it was easy to imagine the answer could be found in simply achieving whatever it took to get rid of the immediate problems.

Once I was convinced the meaning of life lay in Christ I heaved a sigh of relief and proceeded to other matters. It was as if, having handed him all my worries about the future, I could concentrate on getting some happiness for the present—and I'd take care of that myself, thank you.

I felt sure that if I married and my husband was successful in business, enough so as to provide freedom from financial worries, I'd be satisfied with life and with myself. We'd have friends, of course, and all other good in life would follow automatically. All the unhappiness connected with growing up, all my dissatisfaction with self, I attributed to lack of things. Made-over, hand-me-down clothes were, I thought, the source of my self-consciousness and feelings of inferiority. If only I could have dressed as well as other girls! If I had money to spend, could eat lunch in the cafeteria instead of out on the lawn, or could go to the show every Saturday afternoon instead of once in a while.

Today, of course, a great many young men and women are far more mature in their thinking, more aware of the world around them, than I was. They see that all poverty is bad, all deprivation ought to be done away with, all inequities righted. I saw only my own poverty, my own deprivation, and was intensely aware of my own desires. I think I was fairly average. Even the nominal faith I possessed at that time, with its stress on morals and ethics and occasional reminders of eternity waiting sometime (at the end of a long life), could not keep me from fastening the larger part of my thinking on getting a better life—materially.

It took a long, long time to discover that simply having enough of everything did not bring happiness or make me the person I wanted to be. It was not a big enough goal. I feel sure that even if all their goals were realized, and all social inequities abolished, today's eager young crusaders will, in the end, find it is not enough. Getting rid of all the unjust situations in life is not the means by which self-identity is found.

My own situation as a young woman was complicated by the fact that I really didn't like myself very well. It wasn't simply identity I looked for, but something within myself, something other than just what I was, which I would accept as being worthwhile. The identity I looked for had to be worth being.

The temptation here is simply to dump all the blame for my poor self-image onto my parents and let it go at that. It wasn't my fault, it was some lack in their relationship with me that caused the problem. That's partly true, since we do think of ourselves, especially as small children, in terms of our parent's attitude toward us. But it's only part of the story. For whatever reasons—parents, friends, teachers, my own awareness of my shortcomings—I wasn't confident of my own worth as a person, and I tried in varied ways to become the person I wanted to be.

It would be true, though it sounds harsh and was certainly painful, to say I was forced again and again to abandon any hope of identity through money—or social importance—or financial success. Also I began to see that while I wasn't what I wanted to be, still I wasn't what I had been. Something was happening, not in my surroundings or my situation, but *in me*. I had been worrying about all the wrong things. I had been fearful lest people think I was stupid rather than whether or not my behavior justified the term. I had wanted to be liked, and never stopped to think about liking others. Being regarded as one of the best students in school was more important to me than actually doing the best work I was capable of. But now I could stop my wrong worrying. In my new awareness of myself as a person belonging to Christ, I saw others around me in a new light—they were his also, and so it followed that they must be worth knowing. People began to appear in clearer, sharper colors.

Most important of all, when I forgot to think about myself and how I was doing and was absorbed in interests outside myself, things went better. I liked myself more. A sense of wholesome shame in my conceited

41 / *The Unwanted Self*

absorption in self came to help me climb out of the rut. More and more, as the world around me commanded my interest for its own sake—not for its effect on me— the very happiness and acceptance of my own identity I had been frantically looking for came about.

That old distaste for myself is still there at times. I suppose we never really get rid of old emotional stances, though they do fade.

One woman I know felt distaste for herself even more acutely. By the time she was forty, her life had been a dreary procession of failures in every area. She had failed as a daughter, as a friend, as a wife, and could not even hold a job. Lost in misery and self-loathing, she finally tried going to church as a last, desperate attempt to salvage something from disaster. She responded to Jesus Christ as one who would welcome her, love her, accept her just as she was. Her conversion was all emotion. She wept, noisily and with no thought of appearance, when she realized that here at last was release from the burden of guilt that had made her physically, as well as emotionally, ill.

I had felt rejected, awkward, unacceptable because all the "beautiful people" I knew seemed to have the things I wanted and didn't have. My friend felt rejected because she'd failed at everything she had tried to do. She had a clearer picture of herself than I did, but we were alike in our distaste for the selves we were.

Just as my Christian life was a gradual process of growing and learning, of discovering realities which made nonsense out of my muddled ideas, she learned too. She found that her mind, as well as her emotions, needed to be changed, and she learned to think about the issues of life rather than responding immediately and emotionally to each impression.

Another friend, a man, accepted Christ as the final step in a logical progression of steps. His conversion was primarily intellectual—he recognized the sovereignty of God, almost as one would see the inescapable logic of the law of gravity once it was explained. Later on his emotions too were involved, but at first the change in him was primarily one of thought, not feeling. Before he was a Christian he was a happy pagan, taking life and love very lightly and not at all troubled by questions of morals. The scruples came with his knowledge of God.

As differently as the three of us came to know Christ, as varied as were our experiences and temperaments, we each found in the Christian faith the one thing needed to fill our emptiness. We found our own identity as persons loved, accepted by Christ and assured by him of our value. We are not at all alike, and since God is the maker of all variety, his work in our lives is not at all the same. There is one experience we have in common, however: the new selves we are growing into are there because of will, not simply emotion. And, too, we have discovered that living like a Christian isn't automatic.

When we are tired, or coming down with a cold, or discouraged, or sometimes just generally ill at ease, we slip back into the emotional groove of that old self. We all have a habitual set of mind, an attitude toward ourselves and toward others which is the sum total of all we were without Christ. It is made up of all the impressions, ideas, prejudices, and experiences, and thoughts of life on the natural level.

The man who came to Christ out of a careless, not particularly unhappy worldliness slips back into that attitude at times. He doesn't like it, naturally. All its shabbiness is now plain to him; but it comes creeping in when his vitality is down. The friend who found release from the guilt and failure which had dogged her so long finds that when she is a bit "under," that old self-loathing returns. The habitual set of mind I fall into when I'm tired or ill is one of self-distrust and fearfulness. The fear is formless, about nothing—just there. Circumstances give it an object, and I become afraid of some particular possibility. Where once I was afraid of being thought of no account because I had less money than others, now I fear being found wanting in other ways.

I can see that by the time one is an adult there are bound to be some problems, some uncertainties, some scars, and certainly a share of the fear and guilt common to everyone. No one escapes. No one ever becomes a Christian without bringing the unhappy burden of an unwanted self, an identity not comfortable to live with. Living as a Christian *is* a process of gaining one's own identity. But before that can begin, and while it is going on, the old, unwanted, unlovely self must be dealt with. We will never get rid of it completely—not in this life—but we can certainly starve it into submission.

The Naked I / 44

This old self requires a lot of nourishment. It lives and swells and grows heavy only with lots of attention. As a matter of fact, it was born originally out of introspection, a deep concern with one's own self, and it exists only on self-absorption. The most effective manner of doing it in, therefore, is to deprive it of the attention which is its life. In order to do this, we have to acknowledge the condition and call it by name. For instance, I must say to myself at such times, "I am cross and irritable and imagine people are slighting me because I'm tired. I know my thinking isn't reasonable, but I know why it isn't—and this will pass when I feel better." There is no point in praying for spiritual renewal when one is physically exhausted, or in trying to feel close to God at a time of emotional depletion. God does not blame us for being tired or depressed or ill—these are states to which our physical existence is prone.

Whatever the pre-Christian set of mind is—whether it is an unpleasant conviction of one's own inferiority, or a sudden chill fear that life is meaningless, or a distaste for spiritual duties and a couldn't-care-less attitude, the first thing is to call it by name, recognize it for what it is, and then turn away from it.

Such a remnant of the old life is a temptation, like any other temptation, and you don't fight that enemy by concentrating on it, only by starving it. I don't agree with the advice, often given in Christian writings, simply to "pray about it." That emphasizes the strength and power of the problem. Of course that doesn't mean that one should ignore the problem.

Prayer is certainly effective—but only if it leads *to* something. Just wallowing in agony and reiterating the same petitions will not do one thing for this particular problem. It *thrives* on attention, even the attention we give it in prayer.

God gives generously when we ask, but never without our cooperation. He doesn't have to be persuaded that we need help. Having prayed, we must act—that is, obey what we know of his will.

During the months when I was struggling desperately not to have a nervous breakdown, following our daughter's death and a cross-country move, I found that prayer was only the beginning of a healing process. I did pray, following Paul's advice to the Philippians which I read over and over again. Paul told them to bring all their worries, however small, to God and assured them that the peace of God which cannot be understood would keep their minds and hearts. But that was not all. "Here is a last piece of advice," he added. "If you believe in goodness and if you value the approval of God, fix your minds on whatever is true and honorable and just and pure and lovely and praiseworthy."

That is what I tried to do. At times, the effort to drag my thoughts away from myself and my fears was like those nightmares when you must run but your legs are like lead. But slowly, uncertainly, I persisted. Nor did it end there, with the battle fought out only in my mind. We're total beings, body as well as mind and spirit, and I knew I couldn't just *think* myself out of morbidity. I had to act myself out. I embarked on a frenzied program of painting and papering, so that I went to bed at night too exhausted to lie awake with my anxieties.

The trouble with many of us is that we divide things God meant to be a unity—body and soul, spiritual and secular, believing and obeying. There are people who believe that going to Bible study groups is a spiritual activity, so they go to as many as possible and are gently pitying toward those spiritually gauche persons who help with the church dinners or work for the Red Cross or paint the Sunday school furniture. Reading the Bible and praying—and, of course, witnessing— are, for them, spirituality. I thought so too for a long time. But when I needed help and read the Bible, it kept pointing me to action. Most of what Jesus said was about how we ought to behave; Paul consistently finished off every letter with a long portion which amounts to good advice for living. There were frequent commands to do our work well, so I added that to the passage about thinking on what is good and right. It meant I must be active, both mentally and physically, in order for God to help me. I recommend this dual program for anyone trying to climb out of the slough of despondency.

After you have prayed, go and do something else. *Do something.* If you are physically exhausted, get some rest and refreshment, even if it's only changing from the wearying job to something else for awhile. If you have a cold or are ill, do whatever is necessary to feel better—get medication or go to bed. Sometimes I find I am feeling vaguely uneasy, unhappy with myself and there isn't a thing I can put my finger on. At such times nothing refreshes me so much as going off by myself to poke around in antique shops. It wouldn't do for everybody, but it suits me. Whatever you can do to refresh your spirits, do it. And no nonsense about self-discipline, or "I couldn't possibly take the time," because to do what one must do to regain a positive attitude *is* self-discipline.

There is great strength in simply doing a good job of work. Adam and Eve were given work to do, and the "thorns and thistles" didn't become part of it until after they had disobeyed God. Work is good. The routine of each day has structure to it that is extremely helpful when one is under a mood. Work needs to be varied, of course, and it doesn't have to be drudgery. Doing the particular job at hand often is the much needed substitute for that slump into the old habitual self. But *we* must decide.

The reality we are going toward in our Christian lives is not a "natural" thing, as our physical existence is natural, or as our instincts or nerves or emotions are natural. It is a given life, something imparted to us by Christ and with Christ. He is reality, himself in us, incomprehensible though that is. But this new life will not continue to grow without our active consent and participation.

The shades of emotion and thought that are ours need to be refined and sometimes radically altered by Christ. He will not do it without our consent, and that means making decisions. At times the decision may be seemingly minor—to read this instead of that, to do one's desk work instead of reading a novel, to clean the house instead of brooding in discontent. Whatever needs to be done to shake off the shadows of the mind is usually fairly obvious.

Moods *are* shadows, and the mood that conjures up our old selves is the flimsiest of all. We are closest to reality when we *will* to obey Christ. If his command at this moment is merely to get up and do one's job, doing it is the first step toward the goal: the time when our identity, not fully formed now but growing all the time, will be full-blown and perfect.

5. Identity
Given by God

Nothing in life, it seems to me, is ever as clear-cut as we would like it to be. It is impossible to put into words more than a fraction of our thinking, or to describe what happened, or to convey the kaleidoscopic emotions we experience. This makes writing about one's own relationship to Christ very difficult. Out of the tangle of events, impressions, thinking, feeling, growing, learning, that go to make up the days of our lives, some sort of pattern emerges. I look back, as I think about the question of identity in my own life, and see how *that* incident led to *this* thought, how a sermon or a talk with a friend or a book contributed to the pattern. It all reads so neatly, when I put it down on paper—but it's one dimensional. You must remember that while this was going on all sorts of other processes were taking place too.

I feel I ought to put this down because otherwise the

story of a life moving from illusion to reality, which necessarily must be mainly my own experience, sounds too organized. It was not a case of my getting up each morning and thinking, "Now where did I leave off yesterday in my search for identity? Ah, yes, at *this* point. Now to proceed." As a matter of fact, my thinking about identity was just one bubble that broke, occasionally, on the surface of my mind. There were a lot of other bubbles, and a lot of stirring around going on underneath. But it *was* going on.

One of the bubbles that broke was the realization that there was no one pattern for a "standard" Christian. As I read the Bible and thought about the fascinating variety of personages within its pages, from the patriarchs of pre-history like Abraham and Isaac to the self-revealing Paul, whose letters show us his intense passion as well as his intellect, I began to get a glimpse of what God is doing in human lives. These men and women of the Bible were all so different, yet there was no hint of any attempt to make them leave their individuality or conform to a set pattern. In each one God worked in a different way.

There was Jacob, cautious and yet always an opportunist; Joseph, the perfect gentleman and perhaps a bit of a prig, arousing hatred and envy in his brothers by his goodness; Moses, a man larger than life—oversize temper, oversize faith; Joshua, a supreme strategist; Aaron, the very prototype of the ecclesiastical diplomat. And Paul—passionate, sometimes arrogant, often vulnerable and compassionate. What a fascinating variety!

This discovery was most reassuring, since growing

up had been for me largely a matter of conforming, whether I liked it or not. My parents required a standard of behavior that often seemed meant to eradicate any individuality my brothers and I had. Leon didn't like parsnips and Russell hated spinach; but they ate parsnips and spinach (though protestingly).

School made further demands. I played baseball during recess—grimly, reluctantly, hating every moment of it—because everybody played baseball. Games bored me; I would much rather have climbed trees or told stories to the smaller children, but all growing girls and boys must play games so I did. Life seemed to consist of giving up little bits and pieces of oneself in order to be accepted by various individuals and groups necessary to social living.

But how had I ever come to have the idea that all Christians must be alike, as if cranked out of a sausage machine? Or that God was just like my parents, only more so? I thought about some of the Christians I had known who *were* pretty much alike, and whom I had found dull. Was that God's plan, or something mistakenly imposed by people as befuddled as I had been?

While I was proceeding along this path in my study of the Bible, my husband and I were getting to know a group of Christians far different from the stereotypes I had found so uninteresting. These people were alike only in one thing—their devotion to Christ and their serious commitment to him. They were as varied a group as one could gather together if there had been an effort to pick "one of each kind" for a sampling.

It was becoming apparent that God has as many identities to give as there are people.

Each tentative step as a Christian, each new adventure with Christ, showed me that leaving my "old habitual self" behind did not make me just like everyone else. Quite the contrary. It made me *me*. I found this out in many ways, and the process is still going on. As I learned to drop my guard, for instance, and accept others at face value without deciding ahead of time they would either not like me or be a threat to me, I found myself happy and relaxed in my friendships. The sullen, suspicious Eileen, the one I didn't like, was sloughed off like a winter coat when spring comes.

When I ignored the self-pitying voice inside, which told me to be cautious about inviting people to dinner because I didn't have elegant china or silver, and gave some dinner parties and potlucks, inviting people simply because I liked them, I discovered the joy of being free of self-consciousness. In this new, relaxed frame of mind I realized just how much I had squeezed myself into a mold, how cramped and uncomfortable it had all been. The mold was, of course, my impression of what would please whatever group I was with.

"I wonder what I ought to say about . . . they seem very sophisticated, I mustn't be too naïve about their jokes . . . pretty stiff crowd, serious discussion of world affairs is the approach here . . ." You can see how exhausting it was. Amazingly enough, I began to like the new self I was getting to know for the first time. I'd been hiding behind various masks for so long, I really hadn't been too well acquainted with myself.

These new ways of living didn't come all at once, of course. As the changes took place I was aware that the fuel, so to speak, to walk this new path came from God. I was not doing it on my own. Yet I was never so much my own self as now, allowing Christ to break down the walls and tear off the masks I'd been hiding behind.

It seems to me now that one of the greatest gifts God gives to us when we put our lives in his hands is the gift of relaxation. How wonderful to lose the tenseness, the tightly stretched apprehension I had been acquiring all my life! For years I had been trying to conform to some image or pattern which would meet with approval. This necessarily led to intense intro-spection. How should I look, speak, smile, in order to be accepted? Would they like me, or would I be rejected? Should I say what I thought, or what teach-ers, friends, club leaders, wanted to hear? Could I *ever* be honest?

When I mention thoughts like these to groups, all sorts of people come and tell me they've felt the same way. Why? Where did such self-consciousness come from; how did we all get into such a state? For an-swers, we always go back to beginnings, and for the answer to this human problem we must look far, far back.

Much, much more happened in the story of Adam and Eve than appears at first reading. Not just an estrangement from God, but a blurring of the self-knowledge which *is* identity. The first event that took place after Adam and Eve disobeyed God and struck out on their own (for that is what lay behind the eating of the fruit—distrust of God's care, and desire to gain a knowledge of themselves apart from God) was their sudden awareness that they were naked. Since they immediately took steps to clothe themselves, I take it that they didn't like what they saw. Their new self-knowledge was a sad knowledge, a realization that they were totally inadequate to face God. That was the beginning of a history that led to an ever dimmer view of God and with it a corresponding loss of identity.

It may be an oversimplification to say that the whole history of man is the sorry tale of his attempts to find an identity, to build something in life apart from God, but it seems to me that is a large part of it. How many substitutes there are for knowing oneself as God's creature, a being made for fellowship with him! Early man found identity in his tribe; men have looked for it in building kingdoms and nations, or religions. Today we try to find identity in groups of one sort or another, each group having its distinctive modes of living and acting. It can even be observed in the way we dress. How simple to spot the rising young executive with the Madison Avenue image; or the rebellious and anti-establishment man or woman with the long hair, freaky clothing, and grotesque spectacles; or the suburban matron wearing her carefully teased hairdo like a badge of identification!

Just as I had been the captive of inward fears and suspicions which caused me to build a wall around myself, so many people hide behind the image they've

55 / *Identity Given by God*

created. The image is there to protect the poor, vulnerable self from the wounds we all are so afraid of. As I began to relax in the security of knowing God loved and accepted me, and so to discover my true self, that dreadful self-protectiveness drained away.

What happens in the Christian life is really a kind of reversal of the story of the Garden of Eden. There, human identity was lost as Adam and Eve turned from God. Since the only reality lies in God, the only real identity we have comes from him, and we discover ourselves best as we learn to know him. And since he is the author of infinite variety, he never makes us over into carbon copies of each other, but strips away all the false images to reveal the true self.

Jesus assumed his right to give man true identity on several occasions. At the beginning of his ministry, when he first met Peter he said to him, " 'You are Simon, the son of John. From now on your name is Cephas' (that is, Peter, meaning 'a rock.')" The next day he remarked of Nathanael, " 'Now here is a true man of Israel; there is no deceit in him!' " showing that he saw the true nature of the man. Nathanael was just as surprised as we are at finding ourselves open secrets to Jesus.

There are two aspects of the work Jesus does for us and in us. He gives us our true identity (I call you Peter), and he unwinds the tangled mass of protective coverings we have wound about ourselves. To some Jews who believed in him but were clinging to a false notion of their spiritual identity as sons of Abraham he said, " 'Believe me when I tell you that every man who commits sin is a slave. For a slave is no permanent part of a household, but a son is. If the Son, then, sets you free, you are really free!' "

I had been just like those righteous, respectable Jews—trying to make it on my own, and that was sin. Not merely (as I can comfortably assure myself) doing certain forbidden things which I was too cowardly to do anyway, but putting up a false front. As long as I relied on that image, I could never allow my real self to be known. It had to live, stunted and restricted by the limits of the mold. It was a sin, I realized, not to allow the self that God had given me to live and grow.

All this meant change, of course; and change is never without some pain. And yet all through the New Testament I found the same demand for new direction. That's what one does to get off the wrong road, or out of the rut, and I knew it was necessary.

It was also apparent that the identity I was finding in my new relationship to Christ included others. Relationships had always been a problem, but always directed inward. All my questions had been about *their* relationship to me—essentially self-centered. Now I was beginning to see others as people who had needs of their own. Instead of being merely "they," an anonymous mass important only as they related to me, individuals became real people with color and distinction.

So I came into a family—the family of God. I looked around and didn't immediately find myself enchanted with all my new brothers and sisters, but then that's true in any family. We are not allowed to choose. It wasn't long before it became very apparent to me that the identity I now had would be shaped and colored a great deal by family relationships.

These two discoveries about the Christian life—the inevitability and necessity of change, and the importance of relationships—revolutionized my life. But I have also discovered that there is danger in the new life. There is always risk to living, and the Christian life is no exception. It can be slowed, even nullified, by falling into the same old trap that was abroad in Jesus' day here on earth—tying one's self-concept to something other than God.

6. A Case of Mistaken Identity

As I think back over the years I've been a Christian, I recall the many times I was abruptly yanked from the apparent (but false) security of settling down in a cozy little box, with all my opinions and attitudes toward Christianity tucked around me. In the first flush of enthusiasm I thought that all good Christians believed about all things just as did the group of people we had come to know. Their opinions became my opinions.

This comfortable state of affairs continued for a few years. I did not realize how many facets of my particular shading of thought were not from the Bible, nor part of the tradition of Christendom, but were simply of a very small group. Still less did I perceive that many of my attitudes towards other groups of Christians, or certain Christian leaders, were not formed by anything I knew about them. One church figure, in particular, was always spoken of in my circle as if he were a heretic. No one ever *said* anything specific about him, or what he did or what he believed— just the tone of voice was enough. Then at a large church convocation I had occasion to hear that man preach, and out the window went all my prejudices! Whatever the differences between us on matters of church government or other subsidiary areas of life, this man loved Jesus Christ. The strength of his commitment as well as his concern and compassion for the world were clear.

I went home and sat down to think through all the ideas about the proper Christian life and the correct Christian concepts I had unthinkingly accepted.

It was obvious that this man was devoted to Jesus Christ. I had adopted other people's opinions and judgments as my own, without testing to see whether they were true or not. Had I also unthinkingly accepted the criteria of "my group" as divinely sanctioned without investigating for myself? There was certainly a way to find out.

I began to read the Bible with renewed seriousness— not to discover some new truth, but to square what I already *thought* was the truth with God's revelation of himself.

I discovered that the foundation beliefs of our faith are held in common by all Christians. But that was not all. It began to be evident that the wisest and best of men had, for centuries, been unable to agree on many minor points of doctrine. Good men, deeply devoted men, had read the same Scriptures, and come to differing points of view about many things: the best form of church government, the relationship of man to a secular world, modes of living, cultural questions—the list is endless.

Did God accept only those whose theological views were untouched by human fallibility? Must one enter the kingdom of Heaven the same way students get into a university—by passing an entrance exam? I read Paul's words again, "If you confess with your lips that Jesus is Lord and believe in your heart that God raised him from the dead, you will be saved. For man believes with his heart and so is justified, and he confesses with his lips and so is saved" (Romans 10:9, 10, RSV). How fundamental that statement is! No theories of the atonement, no view of the church, no doctrine of man.

And what about Jesus' attitude toward people? Men and women were called into a personal relationship with Jesus Christ as he met them where they worked, or ate dinner with them, or responded to their appeals for help. He asked one man whom he had healed if he believed in the Son of Man. The man replied that if Jesus would tell him who the Son of Man was, he'd believe in him. " 'You have seen him,' replied Jesus. 'It is the one who is talking to you now.' " At that the man said very simply, "Lord, I do believe," and worshiped him. What happened after that we do not know. Did the man become one of Jesus' followers? Or did he pursue his new life there in Jerusalem, believing in Jesus but never learning more of his faith? Whatever he did, his destiny was altered by that one act of faith and we have no right to judge him or decide what his spiritual standing was.

Like the early church —and like every generation of

Christians since then—we find it hard not to succumb to the notion that one's identity as a Christian is established by something other than Christ. Either keeping certain rules, believing a carefully worked out theology, living according to a certain established mode —these are the aberrations we may drift into. And they *are* deviations. They put something other than Jesus Christ in first place, as the determining factor of the Christian life.

Like the church in all times, we tend to make the same wrong turning the Old Testament Jews made. They were meant to find their true identity in their relationship to God. To help them remember their unique calling God gave them reminders—a system of worship and sacrifice, visible symbols and religious and civil laws which marked them off sharply from their neighbors.

As we read their history, we see that almost at once they began to identify with the visible reminders God gave them instead of with him. They found their security and pride in their physical heritage and their distinctive religious ritual. Later they relied on the law. Keeping the law became more and more a matter of the strictest observance. Each law was buttressed and hedged about with supporting regulations to make sure of its sanctity. They were substituting something *they* did for the God who commanded their obedience. Their security, as they identified with it, was more important than God. They had identified themselves with something less than God, the law this time instead of the temple and the sacrificial system.

It's very easy to look back and see how wrong they were, to chart their wrong moves and render our judgment on their failure while congratulating ourselves on our superiority. I've sat in discussion groups many times and noted how comfortable we all felt as we analyzed the blindness of the Pharisees and Sadducees. How perceptive of us to be able to see so clearly *their* failings!

That very smugness and assumption of spiritual excellence is evidence that we, too, tend to fall into the same pit. *Any* self-congratulation means that we've missed the point and are relying on something other than the gracious acts of God in Christ. We have made the dangerous assumption that we are immune to such self-deception; or that we will never fail to please God —a sure sign that both these situations exist.

The visible fragmentation of the church into many segments is partly the result of wrong identification. The New Testament clearly states that Christians are to be patient and forbearing with each other, to refrain from judging each other (the entire fourteenth chapter of Romans spells this out in detail), and that the only criterion for membership in the body of Christ is that of acknowledging him as Lord.

Yet almost from the beginning, Christians have read one another out of the church on the basis of minor theological differences, or because of quarrels over church government or matters concerning food and drink.

This is not to say that the early church councils were not vital to the life and growth of Christian doctrine. They were. But debates over issues aside from from the deity of Christ were never meant to divide. And there is no suggestion in the Bible that a correct theology will get us into heaven. Jesus and his apostles put great stress on attitudes and behavior, as being both the demonstration of our relationship to him and that upon which we will be judged.

"Oh, well," a man said as this very subject was being discussed, "most of the divisions in the church happened long before our time. They're not our responsibility." Later he very heatedly castigated anyone who didn't hold the same view on the first three chapters of Genesis that he did; and he flared into temper when anyone in the group disagreed with his opinions. (It was hard not to disagree with him, as he held strong opinions on everything from the Second Coming to what happened on the second day of creation, and he spoke with the authority of one divinely inspired.) He could not endure discussion on his faith, because he identified—not with Christ as his redeemer and Lord—but with a certain set of propositions *he* had decided were infallible. His faith was not faith at all, but works—he believed himself righteous by virtue of the good work of believing certain things.

Unlike that, however, some sins at least have their origin in some kind of human warmth, even if it is the misplaced good-heartedness which leads a woman to give herself too lightly and casually to men. But the man who believes he has God's last word on every subject is presumptive, taking to himself the very privileges of God. His is a cold, hard, brittle sin which is a problem, though he may not know it, to himself because he will never be open to more truth, thinking he already has it all. And it certainly causes trouble in the church, since those who believe themselves to be in possession of *the* truth are usually sniffing around to see if they can find some deviation from it. When they do—whether it is a wrong view of the sacraments or a preference for modern hymns in calypso rhythm rather than "In the Garden" sung *very* slowly—watch out.

In spite of the irritation such people evoke in me, I feel very real sympathy for them. They are, underneath their brittle exterior, so frightened, so insecure. I was once that frightened and insecure and I remember with what frantic mindlessness I clung to the opinions I had. There had to be *something* I could point to as the justification for myself, and since I was very discontented with what I knew I was, my refuge lay in my "superior" views. I was very touchy, as sensitive as the man who couldn't stand discussion, for to disagree with what I believed was, to my warped thinking, to disagree with me—what I was. I once left a Bible study group very hurt because a man had questioned (in, I thought, a most superior manner) a statement I had made. He was, as I saw it, doubting my ability as a thinker, hence my reliability and ultimately my worth as a person. I fretted over this, and the blow to my self-esteem seemed grievous until, during a subsequent conversation on another matter in which we found ourselves in complete agreement, I discovered he'd forgotten the entire incident.

Becoming a Christian began to put an end to that

self-delusion for me: but not an instantaneous end. We're growing, changing creatures and we don't convert instantly from one mode of being to another. The tendency to be overly defensive and hypersensitive about my point of view clung for a long time. Such an attitude, however, can always become the graveyard of Christian growth. The great danger for many of us as we become Christians is that we will stop short of the good Christ wants us to have, and find our security and our identity not in Christ as our Lord, but in our doctrine about Christ, our mode of living, our keeping of the rules, or our culture.

This attitude utterly negates the very gospel it claims to possess. It will certainly produce extreme frustration, for now of all times it is futile to identify with a particular culture, or a traditional way of living and expressing the gospel. Change is all around us, and no part of our culture is untouched. All the accepted moralities and ethics, not to speak of mere customs, are being questioned.

We are just as faithless to Christ when we equate his gospel, the gospel of the first century, the Middle Ages, and all times, with *our* culture, as we are when we box it neatly into our own tiny theological package. When we insist that the church continue to have everything the way we always have (as if it dated back to Peter and Paul), we usually want to perpetuate the Christian culture we grew up in. What was acceptable to us in the thirties or forties or fifties is clothed with divine sanction for all ages.

To many of those who see all that is phony in society, who question what we've always accepted, it must seem that there is no difference in our eyes between a "proper" order of service, or mode of dress, and matters of morals and ethics. Many people I know do, indeed, equate the two. It is as upsetting to them to see a long-haired college man at church as it is to uncover a case of immorality.

Recently a group of college men and women in a large church began to reach out to the youth of their area. They worked through a coffee house which the church gave them permission to establish; and they had various singing groups which put on programs of contemporary music. A number of today's rebellious, seeking generation have become Christians through this effort. That should have been cause for rejoicing on the part of all concerned Christians. How disappointing it was to find that some of the most "spiritual" members of the church were visibly (and loudly) upset over the whole thing. They complained bitterly about the "undesirables" that were to be seen around the church. By that, they meant young women and men whose manner of dress was strange, whose appearance marked them as "not one of us." All very reminiscent of the Pharisees who sneered that Jesus went about with "tax collectors and sinners."

These modern day Pharisees are finding their identity in one particular cultural expression which they assume to be the only valid Christian expression. They are wrong, and they hurt others by their hard, judgmental attitude. But saddest of all, they have taken their stand on ground which is dissolving beneath their feet, for nothing will stop the moving, fluctuating cultural scene. Jesus Christ remains the same, the gospel remains the same—but our world, and our way of living and putting the faith into practice are always in transition.

Just as we no longer wear the long flowing robes of the first century, nor the bustles and high-button shoes of the nineteenth, so we no longer express our faith quite as they did. Not that we say different *truths*—but we express the eternal truth in contemporary language, as we live the eternal gospel in contemporary situations. Our identity is not with the trappings of the church, however easily and comfortably they fit us, but with the Lord of the universe, timeless, eternal, not imprisoned nor totally defined by any theology in any culture, but Lord of them all.

7. But Don't Change Me!

Change had certainly come into my life. That was all to the good—but as a way of life?

The inevitability of change in the Christian life did not become obvious to me all at once. Nor did the full extent of the alterations Jesus intended to make dawn on me in the beginning. I am still discovering areas I had hardly noticed before which are shabby and run-down, greatly in need of drastic remodeling.

Oh, I understood well enough that committing my life to Christ meant an initial change, and that the words "repentance" and "sanctification" had to do with taking a new direction in life. But I had no idea of the *extent* or the duration of change in my life.

Every time I discover something new or find my thinking has been enlarged by hearing or reading or seeing some new truth, the shock of leaving familiar territory is experienced again. In a sense, life is a process of continually "leaving home." However necessary, it is always painful. Doctors tell us that physical birth is traumatic for the baby; out of the safety of the womb, pushed and pulled and frighteningly constricted and muffled, until emergence and the first breath. Yet to stay in the womb past the allotted time means death.

Perhaps that is why most of us have an innate dislike of change, are uneasy and a little bit tense in unfamiliar surroundings. We say, when we've been away for awhile, "Travel is fun, but coming home is the best part," or "Oh, it's all right to *visit* but I wouldn't want to live there."

In the same way that we prefer familiar places, we prefer familiar patterns of thinking. The old ideas are best. Change is threatening. Even though the one constant factor in everyone's life is change, we all dislike it to some extent.

Everyone has, I suspect, some small corner of himself and his life which he cherishes and protects; it is the one place which must not be touched. Sometimes our little patterns of life by which we maintain continuity and stability are fairly superficial, like always having Post Toasties for breakfast at exactly 8:00, or going every summer to the same vacation spot. These comfortable familiar routines give enough sense of permanence to us to permit flexibility of thinking. New ideas can be considered and accepted because there is no threat to the established habits of living.

Even the most receptive thinker, however, has tucked away somewhere in himself the one untouchable area. It may be his politics, or his religion, or the way he handles his money or treats his wife, but whatever it is, to question it at all would threaten the very fabric of his life. Some people cannot stand any discussion of civil rights; or social action; or liturgical renewal; or sex education in the schools.

There is in most of us a tendency to associate our opinions with our worth as persons, so that any disagreement becomes a personal affront. Part of becoming mature consists of learning that acceptance or friendship doesn't mean thinking alike, and in being secure enough to get along with people whose life style and philosophy are different from ours.

The rigid thinker who is intolerant of any deviation from his values, his opinions, is really not a strong person. He is too unsure of his own values to live without constantly having them reinforced. Even crusaders and creative thinkers who rebel against a society they think too rigid are often just as locked into their own position. The changes they are shouting for are changes *outside themselves*—in the world around and in other people. These changes are often much needed and long overdue. But those who shout the loudest for them bear within, like the rest of us, a little pool of selfhood which seeks to protect itself from alteration.

Whether you are a member of the "establishment" or an angry young militant bent on remaking society, you—like me—are a person who doesn't want to *be* changed, only to effect changes around you. Change my parents, change my children, change my town, my country, the world—but don't change me! Secretly, none of us wants, in this sense, to have to leave home, to be pushed out the door to cope with an alien world, a world which may demand that *we* be the ones to change. The search for identity is sometimes impeded by an unrecognized, but very strong, fear that we may not like our identity when we find it, and an equally strong reluctance to change ourselves.

The gospel is frightening and repelling to many because it says to us, "*You* must change." Most of us are aware that growth is change and that it is necessary. We accept it, with certain inward reservations. We want to know more, to be more intelligent or better looking or more popular or more successful. These, we acknowledge, are good alterations. But the "real me" we are reluctant to submit to the indignity of modification. To acknowledge that my essential self needs altering threatens the sense of worth I have, and I tend to reject the idea. I suppose I may possibly fear, in a wordless, even unthought-out fashion, that any real change in the mysterious entity I call "me" might end in my self being lost or lessened in the process of alteration.

This fear of alteration in my own life is, I have learned (but how slowly and painfully), not compatible with the teaching of the New Testament and must be discarded. I used to think that since I had become a Christian and made the initial commitment to Christ, that was enough change. The future would simply be a matter of doing all the "right" things and avoiding the more obvious sins. What became evident as time went on was that I needed to change attitudes, habits of thinking and reacting—that the emotional climate of my life had to change. Without that I could not do the right things and avoid the wrong ones. My sins had sprung out of what I was, and what I was had to be brought into conformity with the new life Christ had given. He really meant it when he spoke of cutting off hands and plucking out eyes, though he used figures of speech. But such phrases sounded to me as though the Christian life was all a matter of giving up, emptying out—in a sense being reduced.

It was a long time before I was able to understand that when Jesus spoke of being born again, and Paul spoke of Christians as being new creations, or of himself as being dead to the law but alive in Christ, they were not describing men as paler, less colorful, washed-out. Rather they saw them as more vibrant, more potent. Jesus said, "I came to bring them life, and far more life than before."

How could I reconcile that statement with his stern words about entering by the straight gate, cutting off the offending hand, walking the narrow way, or (even more dismaying) losing one's life in order to find it? All of these suggested a rather painful pruning. If one got by without losing a hand or an eye, there was still the hint of scraped knuckles or singed eyebrows. In fact, reading through any of the four Gospels usually left me with extremely mixed emotions. There were so many instances of Jesus' love and concern for people, so many kind and comforting words. But on the next page, sometimes in the very next paragraph, there would be an observation or command which jolted me by its uncompromising demand for perfection, or its

73 / But Don't Change Me!

insistence on total commitment to an impossibly high standard. I usually pinned my hopes on the comforting words and gave up on the hard sayings, shoving them to the back of my mind with the thought that he must have meant them figuratively, which I interpreted to mean "not *really*."

I was wrong. The truth of Jesus' words, both the stern, uncompromising passages and the reassuring and comforting sentences spoken to the poor, the ill, and the grieving, became apparent through experience. By whatever name you call growing older—maturing, experiencing life, having some hard knocks—it has been to me a manifestation of the reliability of the words of Jesus.

Jesus was simply telling us we needed to change. He said, as pointedly and graphically as possible, that we are miserable creatures when we live apart from God; that we *must* change or die, and that the alteration won't be easy but that it will bring unimaginable happiness in the end, worth all the temporary misery and uncertainty.

There are some propositions which can be verified only by experience, not by reasoning. Spiritual truths fall into that category. When Jesus said that the person who wants to save his life will lose it, but that anyone who loses his life for Jesus' sake will find it, he was not contradicting his statement, "I came to bring . . . life, and far more life than before." The element which harmonizes these two seemingly opposite statements is change.

Our ideas of happiness and security are so childish,

so impoverished, that we have to be forcibly yanked free of them before we can experience a fuller happiness, a more genuine security. When I was a little girl I thought that life would be perfect bliss if I could play all day, never have to help with the dishes or do housework, and forget baths. As a teenager all I wanted was to be pretty, popular, and have a date every Friday and Saturday night. After I got married I wanted a house in the East End, a newer car, and a matching living room suite. (The mere thought of the furniture I admired so much then makes me shudder now.)

I am beginning to see (though often very dimly) that what I *thought* was the way to "save my life" even regarding such superficial things as food and clothes, was not worth hanging onto. I had to give it up in order to discover something better. The abundant life Jesus talked about is in the beginning stages for me, and I must remember that the changes he brings do not drain the color out of life—they deepen pastels to glowing hues.

8. The Eye
of the Needle

There are certain phases of my life as a Christian I find uncomfortable, even embarrassing. An acute unhappiness comes over me when I have—again—said or done something mean, shabby, and out of keeping with the faith I profess. As I analyze my emotions at such times, I find not just sorrow for having failed to be perfect, or repentance for having sinned, but rather mortification. My own self-esteem has taken a tumble, because I really thought better of myself than that.

I know, for instance, that as a person continually in need of God's forgiveness I must also be forgiving. It's very easy to think of myself as being big enough to overlook slights or snubs or offensive remarks until I'm slighted or hurt—and then how quickly I flare into wrath. Even when it's contained so that nothing in my manner shows that I'm seething inside, the realization that I'm not as big as I thought is very sobering.

This humiliation is a continuing experience. Not just at the first, when as a new Christian I might have been expected to make many blunders, but again and again I am chagrined at my own failings. In talking with other Christians I find that they, too, feel the same sense of shame at continually falling short of what we know we ought to be.

Our failures may appear to be very petty transgressions, one might almost call them foibles, but each of us knows they indicate serious flaws. My friends may see only an occasional flare of irritation, for instance, but I know the envy or hurt pride which, like an iceberg, hides its bulk below the surface. On these occasions I am angry with myself for two reasons: in my foolish conceit I had pictured myself as beyond such petty transgressions, but now that image has been shattered again. More than that, it means there is still need for me to change. Will the process never end?

These continued failings face me with a dilemma—I need to change because I am a sinner (however distasteful that word is), and because I am a sinner I don't want to admit I need to change. I suspect that all of us are alike in this regard. We need to face the fact that we Christians, though we talk a good game, are frequently busy trying to wiggle out of the necessity of continually submitting ourselves to Christ for correction. We do this by externalizing the problem.

Instead of admitting that we are never going to reach perfection in this life, that we are, basically, sinners who will always need forgiveness, we impute the evil inside us to things outside us.

We all know at least one person whose passion for perfection demands so much of family and friends that they can never come up to it. The most critical woman I know, famed for her caustic remarks about the shortcomings of everyone, is especially quick to comment on a critical spirit in anyone else. She doesn't see herself as extremely critical—just realistic. For years I was supersensitive about people with money— just waiting for them to show some sign of snobbishness or of judging me on the basis of my modest means. Then, with a shock, I saw that I was a snob, telling myself smugly that I was far too intelligent to use money as my standard of worth.

We are all in danger of thinking like this, of seeing in others the very thing we refuse to face in ourselves. It is our way of evading the hard truth Jesus emphasized when he said that we could do nothing apart from him. We keep trying to make it on our own. Jesus, when he spoke those words, had first compared his disciples to the branches of a vine, himself, and told them they would be pruned so they might bear more fruit. Bearing fruit is all right, we think, but pruning —much too painful, we'd rather flourish just as we are.

Jesus meant by this parable that we don't have enough virtue or goodness in ourselves to live the Christian life. We never will. Practice will not make perfect. The new life he gives us is he himself, not a quality he puts into us. We live and grow and acquire identity only in relationship with him. We *say* we know all that, but we are always drifting away a little, always making efforts to "do it myself."

That's why we don't like to admit that we are still weak enough and sinful enough to need forgiving for the same old failures. They are an embarrassment; they don't fit the picture of a spiritual giant, and we dislike seeing ourselves as pygmies.

The result is a very oversimplified view of the nature of man, as well as of good and evil. The righteousness of God, a blazing fire which consumes all that is not good, has been reduced by some to a tuttutting reproof over spiritual sins such as pride, envy, and malice; and the evil that Christ died to crush is seen as nothing more than certain prohibited acts. If we refrain from doing "those" things—from murder to taking a cocktail—we're all right. In this way the extent of wrong within us has been whitewashed. Not inward cleansing, repentance, and change but outward performance, a conspicuous abstinence from proscribed activities—and hey, presto, behold the saint!

When we externalize evil this way, we have simply failed again to find our true identity. After all, my real self—the self Christ died for, the self he means to make perfect—is all of me including what's wrong with me. I was always meant, as all Christians are, to know myself as a forgiven sinner. A forgiven sinner *in the present tense*. Not I was, but *I am* a person given identity by God, a still somewhat marred and imperfect identity only partially visible and clouded by grievous faults.

Eventually, we are told by the New Testament, the disorders and aberrations in us will all be gone and we will be truly what we were intended to be. But now, here in this life, we are still far short of perfection. Jesus told his disciples to forgive each other seventy times seven, which surely implies the continuing presence of wayward human nature. Perfect people do not need forgiveness. The constant reminder that we are "in Christ," that the new life we lead is a given life, not an inherent one, ought to keep us aware of our own fallibility.

We are still in the process of becoming, our identities are still being hammered out. We need a realistic appraisal of ourselves as Christians—not a rosy-hued view that glosses over the truth about our errant human nature and pretends we're "such lovely people," but a hard-headed look. We have only begun to discover who we really are, to know we are worthwhile and have value because Christ values us. But our identity is still partial, and we are bumbling, faulty, sinful human beings on our way to something better.

The unrealistic view of ourselves shows up quite often at testimony meetings which sometimes become a little series of success stories. People tell how God showed them the error of their ways, or changed their lives, or helped them overcome some bad habit, all with the implication that whatever the problem was, it's over—they've arrived. And if there are people present who suspect it's not quite that simple, they are afraid to admit their own continuing struggling with besetting sins for fear everyone will put them down as hopelessly unspiritual.

The moment we depart from a clear-sighted view of ourselves as forgiven sinners (but still sinners), we become unrealistic not only in our estimate of ourselves but in our knowledge of God and of the world. We can see this happening all around us; sometimes we realize with a jolt we have done it ourselves. Whenever Christians are harsh and judgmental, turning critical eyes on one another, we have forgotten who we ourselves are. Forgiven sinners don't judge others—they know too well how easily they fall into sin. Not that there is a light-minded disregard of wrong; but compassion not judgment, concern and efforts to help rather than criticism, are the response.

In the Sunday school class to which I belong, taught by the Reverend Henk S. Vigeveno, we studied recently the book of James. At two points this very subject—our reluctance to face our identity as forgiven sinners —came up. In the first chapter James said that God does not tempt us. "A man's temptation is due to the pull of his own inward desires, which can be enormously attractive. His own desire takes hold of him, and that produces sin." Later he wrote, "But what about the feuds and struggles that exist among you— where do you suppose they come from? Can't you see that they arise from conflicting passions within yourselves?"

Mr. Vigeveno pointed out that the root of the trouble is *within us,* and we are without excuse. We can't put all the blame on society, or our parents, or unjust teachers, or faulty friends, or even on the devil. *We* are still imperfect, and we have within our natures tendencies which, if not checked and disciplined by submission to Christ, will cause trouble.

81 / The Eye of the Needle

These lessons always disturb some of us greatly. People protest, "But look at the Communists, how awful they are . . . look at the hippies, irresponsible and dirty . . . look at the worldly people sitting in nightclubs and drinking too much . . . look at—look at—look at." We have externalized sin. *Not me, Lord, but those people out there who do dreadful things. Sin is what they are doing—and see how impeccable I am, how virtuous my behavior, how pure and correct is my demeanor.*

At the conclusion of the lesson on James's remarks about our "feuds and struggles," the discussion was illuminating. Some people were quick to say that, after all, we knew certain things were wrong for Christians and we should "stand up for our convictions." One woman asked plaintively, "But don't you think we *have* to have standards, and we just have to let people know when they're not right?"

The trap is always there; no one is free of the temptation to impute the sinfulness in human nature to something outside. Just the other day a much younger Christian, one of the anti-establishment members, demonstrated the same error. He belongs to a large segment of younger Christians who might be called neo-fundamentalists. They dislike everything about the style of older Christians. They don't like our church services, our standards, the way we look—and they show it. They tend to wear long hair and beards and are proudly shabby in dress. They talk a lot about love and refer to each other as "brother" and "sister," but they are—though they don't know it—an anti-establishment establishment. You've got to look like them to be really spiritual. The young man I mentioned is a classic case of the Christian who thinks he *was* a sinner and is now a saint. He advised one of his friends, a girl, to give up wearing make-up and miniskirts. It wasn't spiritual!

Many Christians in my generation, however, are the elderly conterpart of this young man. They don't like the free, unstructured services of the modern young Christian, and they show it. They don't like the strange new music, and even if the words are from the Psalms the rhythm seems irreligious. There is a great gap between "Leaning on the Everlasting Arms" and the calypso Lord's Prayer, and never the twain shall meet. These older Christians believe short hair for men is a sign of Christian rectitude and next to it, as far as godliness is concerned, is "proper" dress. It's all right to be high style or to wear suits whose distinctive lapels speak of the custom tailor, but not acceptable to dress with the originality the younger set prefers.

It's really very funny, and very sad all at the same time. To some Christians, sin lies in drinking, smoking, dancing, and related pastimes. To others it is belonging to the wrong political party or believing differently about baptism or the Second Coming; to others it is belonging to the wrong denomination; and to some young Christians coming up, it is being affluent (unless the rich older generation gives all its wealth to them) or wearing expensive clothes or having your hair done at the beauty parlor or just not looking like they do.

When we take such an attitude, we are like the ducks in Hans Christian Andersen's tale of the ugly duckling. When we see a swan, we say, "He doesn't look like us—let's peck him to death."

I'm constantly tempted to indulge in a little pecking. After all, serious consideration of my neighbor's faults keeps me from having to face my own. I think James was writing to me—to all of us—when, at the conclusion of his stern warning about the danger of spiritual pride and the need for humility, he finished:

> Never pull one another to pieces, my brothers. If you do you are judging your brother and setting yourself up in the place of God's Law; you have become in fact a critic of the Law. Yet if you criticize the Law instead of obeying it you are setting yourself up as judge, and there is only one judge, the one who gave the Law, to whom belongs absolute power of life and death. How can you then be so silly as to imagine that you are your neighbor's judge?

9. The Double
Face of Change

*L*eft to ourselves, we all tend to be provincial—to assume that the way *we* live, the style in which we worship God and express our faith, has universal validity. As a young woman growing up in a small church located in a small town, I assumed that our standards were God's standards in every detail. Naturally, the first time I left home and discovered a wider world (and, I must admit, a more interesting world than I had known), those particular measuring rods for life were seen to be inadequate. Not necessarily bad, or wrong, but certainly not all-encompassing as I had thought them to be.

It was not the Christian faith itself that was called into question, merely the manner of life I had always assumed to be Christian. Matters of dress, deportment, entertainment, and other rather peripheral items were often regarded with more seriousness than larger questions. There was plenty of prejudice, unkindness, exclusiveness and general human cussedness in that church, as there is everywhere. We were wrong in our emphasis, not because these wrongs were present, but because we ignored them while we paid great attention to trivial issues. We were like the people Jesus accused of being meticulous in their observance of small matters—like tithing mint, anise seed or dill, and cummin, while they neglected the things that were really important, "the weightier matters of the law, justice and mercy and faith" (Matt. 23:23, RSV).

Some people in the church were merciless in their criticism of a girl who wore too much make-up or dressed flamboyantly, but they ignored the squabbles and backbiting that went on. I don't believe any of the leading men smoked—at least not openly. That wouldn't have been "spiritual." Yet nothing was ever said in the church about the barely honest business deals several of them were noted for. And even if they weren't so culpable in their ethics, the preoccupation with appearances made for extremely dull meetings.

Like many others, as my husband and I saw the fallacy of living according to the niggling little distinctions of life which seemed to have nothing to do with real issues, we left the church for a while. Our knowledge of our faith was sketchy at best, and in losing interest in the church we were not abandoning Christianity, merely leaving an expression of it which was inadequate.

Because we did not look for a more vital way of living as Christians we simply drifted off into a kind of limbo for a few years. We became very worldly in our attitudes, and I use the word "worldly" to indicate where our interests were. The New Testament writers described such lives as ours during those years in various ways. Jesus told stories illustrating the attitude; Paul sometimes called it being "carnally minded," or "spiritually blind." In our experience, being worldly was the combination of an avid self-centeredness with flippant tolerance of a morality we once would have thought quite shabby. Slowly, insensibly, in our revolt against what we rightly saw to be a legalism that stressed minor matters more than true goodness, we were losing touch with the Christian faith itself, the reality behind all the rules and finicking distinctions.

When we became aware of the distance we had traveled away from any serious commitment to God, it was mainly because the shallow, pseudo-sophistication of our lives was even more disappointing than the narrowness of the church we had once been part of. Again, a radical change took place—this time in the direction of wholehearted commitment to Christ. The people through whom this new life was mediated to us were in a large church in Los Angeles, and into the life of that large church we flung ourselves with great energy.

Because the preaching and the teaching were very, very good, and the Christians we met were extremely well-informed about their faith, we plunged into Bible studies, discussion groups, and Sunday school class with the same fervor we had once felt only for a nightclub with an excellent floor show. The change was necessary and good. But we were in danger of making an old mistake all over again—adopting the point of view and customs of our new group *as if* they were the apex of all human thinking and doing.

We were not allowed, however, to remain in that comfortable but treacherous state very long. Where some lives proceed serenely, even-paced, ours were shifted, shaken and dislodged by changes in every area. In a few years' time Russ tried several new business ventures, underwent major surgery, our two daughters had polio and, as a result, we were hard-pressed financially. Each experience tested the assumptions we had made about our faith.

The good these alterations brought was not immediately apparent, but it was very real. The primary good that came to me in experiencing many changes in life was becoming more sure of my identity as a person *in Christ* rather than in any lesser sense. I might have settled for a being a "pillar in the church" in one small group. That in itself would have been all right, except for the accompanying and inevitable temptation to equate that group's standards with God's standards. That was made impossible by a move across country which brought us into close relationship with another church, where they did things differently than we had been used to—but they were worshiping and serving the same God.

It would also have been easy to settle down into the comfort of an attitude typical of our age group: to like the music, the books, the ways of expressing our faith that had become second nature to us. Our children

Darrell and Donna and their friends made that impossible. Many evenings around the dinner table Russ and I expounded our views of what was right and proper for a Christian, only to have them ruthlessly examined —and sometimes demolished. The experience wasn't comfortable, but it was good.

Our idea that one dressed up to go to church to "honor God" turned out to be an evasion of the real reason—we dressed to impress each other. We admitted that, and convinced our children that dressing to impress each other is probably inevitable, whether one dresses "up," as we did, or wears calculatedly casual clothes, as many of their friends did. Our clothes are one way of saying what we are. That was a mutual and helpful exchange of viewpoints.

On the other hand, many of the easy glosses we had put on difficult Bible passages just didn't hold up. That's what comes of having a son around who is studying theology and a daughter whose thinking goes right to the central point of an issue.

Traveling was always a mixture of delight and discomfiture. It was stimulating and enjoyable to see other parts of the world and to meet people, especially Christians, who lived differently than we did. But our naïve assumption that Americans have the best of everything and do everything in the best possible manner was blown to bits, and *that* was unsettling. We found the vitality of Christ being expressed in the lives of people whose worship service was strange to us, whose culture was utterly foreign, and who showed no evidence at all of feeling deprived because they did not possess the glossy American conveniences of life. When we talked about how we did things in our country, they were politely interested and very kind, but not always impressed.

We soon discovered that most European countries have postal systems as good or better in some ways than ours. Personal service is often better, and of course the underground and subway systems of London and Paris put ours in the dark ages. The fast, luxurious, and always split-second electric trains make suburban living without a car not so difficult as in the United States. As for food, traveling across the United States can be a culinary disaster, unless one spends a small fortune and hunts out the most expensive restaurants. In Europe, we ate at small country hotels and inns and had astonishingly good food, often elegantly served. All in all, the assumption of superiority which we Americans (all unconsciously) tend to have was rudely upset.

Many times when I was beginning to congratulate myself on being a member of my denomination, I met someone of another church body whose intelligence and sensitivity and zeal as a Christian were a rebuke to my smugness. The Christian community in a small town in Japan exhibited a love and concern for each other that we seldom see here. The Lutheran church in Germany runs retreat houses and trains social workers, providing an involvement in the life problems of the community. All over this country there are groups of Christians concerning themselves with the troubles of contemporary society and doing something about them. Small churches, middle-sized or large churches, high and low and liturgical and unliturgical—Christians of all shades of theological posture are carrying their faith into everyday life.

The temptation to settle down in a comfortable groove and burrow into a cozy niche that just fits me is always present—and always being dealt with. It is as if Christ is continually having to nudge me back into the main road as I drift off into little dead-end streets. My identity, and my way of life, must be found in him and not in anything less, even if it is a good thing in itself. The bumping and nudging that put me back into the main road are sometimes bruising, hurting experiences. They always involve change. Just as I am in great danger of mistaking the situation I am in, or the pleasant life I'm leading, or the congenial group of friends surrounding me for the identity I ought to find only in Christ, change comes and forces me to recognize the fact that in none of these good elements of life do I find my ultimate identity.

That kind of change is good, though painful. It's a little bit like always leaving home. We are, as the writer of the Epistle to the Hebrews said, destined for a heavenly city and must be restless until we reach it. But we are always tempted to settle for something less, to put down roots right here. So we dislike the changes that alter our comfortable niches. But we ourselves by our tendency to stop short of the best, make those changes necessary. Without the implacable weight of shifting events and fluctuating circumstances which force me to adapt, learn, and to grow, I'd just

91 / *The Double Face of Change*

plop down and make myself comfortable. The alterations in life which prevent that from happening are
good, even though they may involve painful readjust-
ments.

There are, though, changes which we all sense to
be sad, changes which bleed the joy and brilliance out
of life. The sense of expectancy, the wonder of new-
ness with which we viewed the world about us as children, didn't last long. The mystery and discovery of
childhood vanished with childhood; and though growing up brought its own good, something delightful was
lost. All through life the present good is being shifted,
worn out, drained away. I can remember many good
times with friends, evenings of hilarity and good fun.
Picnics and barbecues and potluck dinners were the
order of the day for growing families. Some of these
friends are gone, some have moved away and some
(saddest of all) have just quietly drifted apart.

When I go back to the small town in which I grew
up, now considerably larger, I am a stranger on the
once familiar streets. I can recall quite clearly the
experiences of my childhood and the emotions that accompanied them—but I can't *feel* them any more. I've
changed and can't go back.

Even the physical alterations in our surroundings
have an effect of sadness, however convenient they
may be. The arrogantly towering highrise buildings,
the freeways slashed through mountains, the shopping
centers displacing orchards are all necessary, we assure ourselves. "Progress is inevitable," we may sigh,
with a secret longing for the shape of the landscape as

it used to be, the city skyline unbroken by skyscrapers, and the orchards stretching away to the foothills. We call this emotion "nostalgia," and are a little embarrassed by it because we don't know what to do with it.

Sometimes we experience a quiver of fright at the alarming rapidity with which our world is being changed. Of course it would be dreadful above all things to bemoan old times, for we would certainly be considered old fogies by the traditionless young. But all the time there is a nagging conviction that *some* of the advantages of the past are gone forever. Progress brings many good changes, but not without wiping out ways of life that had their own unique good.

Even in the first century A.D., when progress moved at a snail's pace, the alterations suffered in life were the cause of pain. Paul recognized this when he wrote regarding present distress and suffering, linking *our* limitations and incompleteness to the physical world:

> The world of creation cannot as yet see reality, not because it chooses to be blind, but because in God's purpose it has been so limited—yet it has been given hope. And the hope is that in the end the whole of created life will be rescued from the tyranny of change and decay, and have its share in that magnificent liberty which can only belong to the children of God!
>
> It is plain to anyone with eyes to see that at the present time all created life groans in a sort of universal travail. And it is plain, too, that we who have a foretaste of the Spirit are in a state of pain-

93 / *The Double Face of Change*

ful tension, while we wait for that redemption of our bodies which will mean that at last we have realized our full sonship in him.

The tyranny of change and decay—universal travail —painful tension—this is the condition of our world, and our lives, and we would be insensitive indeed not to feel sorrow because of it. Though the Bible does not give us a blueprint of heaven, nor draw pictures of the future we call "eternity," certain convictions come to me as a result of reading the New Testament, especially 1 Corinthians 15.

Paul ended that marvelous discourse on the Resurrection (which is really a discussion of the nature of reality) by assuring his readers, "Be sure that nothing you do for him [God] is ever lost or ever wasted." The God who never loses, never lets anything good be wasted, can be trusted, it seems to me, to keep safely *everything* in this life that is worth keeping. We seem to lose much. The freshness of childhood, the enthusiasm of youth, are gone like a sigh. In the kaleidoscope of life friends leave, relationships deteriorate, and we are always conscious in our most happy moments of their transitoriness. We know what the "tyranny of change and decay" is, and no human ecstasy is without the sorrowful reminder that however lovely, the present joy is very fragile. The last of C. S. Lewis's letters included in the collection edited by his brother was written a few weeks before his death. It cannot be read without an aching pang: "Yes, autumn is really the best of the seasons; and I'm not sure that old age isn't the best part of life. But of course, like autumn, it doesn't *last*."*

That is the universal human experience—it doesn't last. But our longing for permanency, our distaste for death in all its forms, even the small, insignificant death of pleasant friendship or the serenity of a summer must surely indicate that somewhere there is permanency. The present good which is gone so quickly is not snuffed out, but it passes into eternity where we will one day find it again.

And that brings me to the second conviction about the restoration of good and the eventual reversal of the tyranny of change and decay, and again I owe it to Paul. In the same fifteenth chapter of 1 Corinthians, in trying to convey something of the reality of the Resurrection, Paul wrote, "For I assure you, my brothers, it is utterly impossible for flesh and blood to possess the kingdom of God. The transitory could never possess the everlasting."

Flesh and blood—the transitory. We know that is true for our bodies are destined to become dust. But the kingdom of God he writes about lies in the very area which now, to so many, *seems* ephemeral. You can't grasp thoughts, emotions, relationships between people, as you can the body. You can't confine in one place that which is spiritual, as you can put a table or a chair in one spot. Everything which now appears to be so solid is capable of destruction. Fire, water, wind, and simply the passage of time can mutilate and

*Letters of C. S. Lewis, W. H. Lewis, ed. (New York: Harcourt, Brace and World, 1966), p. 308.

destroy our houses, furniture, and our bodies—but they can *do nothing* to obliterate our real selves. And everything we value the most, our happiest times and deepest joys, are part of the spiritual world which is everlasting. Bodies are transitory—spirits are eternal.

"Be sure that nothing you do for him is ever lost or ever wasted." And we can be equally certain that no good thing worth keeping is ever lost or wasted. We can be sure that the double face of change—bringing new good into our lives and at the same time taking away present joys, bringing new maturity and insight and sensitivity along with sagging chins, arthritic joints, and sluggish circulation—will itself be altered. The dark side of change will disappear when all the real good we have ever known will be ours. *That's* heaven.

10. Identity
in Relationships

When I committed my life to Christ, I felt I had discovered for the first time my real self—who I really was. I knew I was of value because God loved me. When I thought of my relationship with God, I thought of Jesus Christ and then of myself either praying, or reading the Bible. My idea of a relationship with God was of myself in a solitary state, communing with him. This was a handy concept, since it had absolutely no connection with the rest of my life.

After a while, I preferred to visualize myself praying rather than reading the Bible. Praying—conversing with God—*was* the relationship, while Bible reading was more like reading letters; the words were his, but print made them somewhat impersonal. Furthermore, Bible reading often produced a strong conviction that I ought to conform to its standards, accompanied by guilt as I became aware of my shortcomings. I found this uncomfortable. The Bible was full of stringent demands regarding my relationships with others. How much nicer to concentrate on my fellowship with God, in terms of what was called "daily devotions." When those went well, and I prayed fluently and had lovely feelings, I felt quite spiritual and was sure I was very close to God.

The trouble was, these times of prayer and devotion were so much affected by my association with people. I found it very difficult to assume the proper spiritual posture for prayer when I had been disagreeable to my husband, cross with my children, or offended by my friends. Worst of all, the constant pressure of getting everything done at home and arriving at an appointment on time not only made me less than serene, but positively cross.

One day I rushed into a young mothers' meeting late, flurried, and out of sorts. My friends had saved a seat for me at the luncheon table and I slid into it without a smile. They all looked at me and immediately made soothing noises, which infuriated me. After I had calmed down a bit, the depressing thought came that my reaction had been stronger because I was humiliated at being in need of soothing, at not being always on top. How could a day that began with prayer have been such a disaster by noon?

Gradually and reluctantly the realization came that there was a very close connection between how I got along with others and my relationship with Christ. How annoying! To have the purity, the spirituality of my times alone with my God interfered with, even altered, because of the pettiness of everyday life. It ought to be the other way around, I thought. The serenity and the sheer goodness of time spent in prayer ought to make a difference in all my relationships.

That thought, unplanned, unbidden, was a shock. It was quickly followed by another: prayer and meditation *had not* made much of a difference in the way I treated other people. Perhaps that was why so many associations, untouched by any new sensitivity or kindness from beyond myself, thrust themselves and their problems into my prayers. It began to look as though the mental picture I had of myself and Christ, in solitary communion, was not quite right.

The identity given to me by God—of myself as his creation, his own child (once far from him but now loved and accepted for Jesus' sake)—was, I concluded, meant to flow over into the whole of life. This may sound obvious to perceptive persons, but it is amazing how many of us are not spiritual enough, or sensitive enough, to see it at once. We have been brought up in the atmosphere of a secular world in which religion is supposed to be a personal matter between oneself and God. It does not follow that that is *all* religion is, but we are not logical people. It's all too easy to assume that if religion — and specifically Christianity — is a personal matter, it is nothing more than that.

Realizing this, I saw what ought to have been obvious from the first, that a great deal of the Bible is concerned with us in our relationships. The entire Sermon on the Mount is about what we do and what we say, as well as how we think. Paul ended every letter he wrote with a series of practical instructions on Christian living. As I thought this over, I began to remember how often my life had been given new direction and how much I had been helped by people, not ideas.

For instance, I wasn't doing too well in my shorthand class in high school until the teacher encouraged me, gave me special attention, and implanted in my thinking the idea that I *could* do well. Now that I look back, I realize that many teachers made a good student out of me and gave me a passion for learning by assuming that I had capacities I wasn't aware of. Their expectations evoked response from me.

I remember vividly the first time it dawned on me that perhaps a capacity for friendship was within me and could be expanded. My first child was just a baby when a friend I had met at church called on me one afternoon, as she often did. I was always delighted to see her—to see anyone capable of adult conversation for that matter—and as she walked in she said, "That's one of the things I like about you, Eileen—you're always so glad to see me."

Until then I had not thought much about friendship, other than to be grateful for it wherever it existed. But with those words I saw, far later than I should have, that friendship was not just something I needed, but something I could give to others. How often I had watched eagerly for signs that I was welcomed, I was accepted. But now I began to see that my attitudes toward others might be helpful to them.

The Bible shows us that we rub off on each other,

we give something, either good and helpful or difficult and even harmful, to everyone around us. But this effect we have on each other is implied (rather than stated directly) by the emphasis on how we get along together, both in Jesus' teaching and in Paul's letters. So I was slow to see the implications. Of course I knew that God wanted me to give myself to him, but I had not reasoned from that point to the necessity of giving myself to others. That I would be needed by them, and in meeting that need in friendship would be also giving myself to God was, to me, a revolutionary thought.

It all sounds pretty simple now, but it was a blinding revelation at the time. More and more I am convinced that spiritual progress usually depends upon our seeing, sometimes with shocked surprise, some simple and basic truth clearly for the first time, rather than having to graduate up to some profound difficult theological pronouncement.

My friend's remark made me aware of another fact —that most of us are looking for some signal from others, the look or smile that says our appearance is welcomed. Words are not enough. Anyone can say, "Hello," but the tone of voice and facial expression that go with the word give it meaning. To be greeted happily and with obvious signs of pleasure tells me a bit about who I am. It says I am a person worth someone else's time and attention, and that builds, though in a very small way, the identity of *me*. Each relationship we have shapes our identity one way or another.

Have you ever noticed that some people call out all

the best in us, and by doing so help us to become more and more what that best is? Others bring out all the worst—or at least they do in me. The very presence of certain people can make me bristle with antagonism or retire into chilly silence. It ought not to be, I know, but that is the way I am (and I suspect we all are). The only means I know of getting over my instinctive reactions is to call upon all my reserves of discipline and social training and thus say, or do, the courteous thing.

And *that* sort of situation shapes my identity too. The negative reactions are a sharp reminder of my own imperfections. I know I need help, that left to myself and without Christ I will live on the lowest possible level. Every time I smile when I feel like growling, or carry on a conversation when I'd rather turn and walk away I am, though I don't analyze it at the time, or even think of it, encouraging and expanding my capabilities for discipline and responsibility. My identity is becoming a little more real, acquiring some depth in that area.

As my attitudes change, my relationships alter also, and the new identity God has given me can grow, take shape and acquire solidity. I see myself not as the gauche, inept person I had been, but as someone liked as a friend, listened to seriously, someone accepted. A self-image is not enough, however, for true identity. It must correspond with what is. The trouble with simply relying on my devotional life, my prayers, as establishing the proper relationship with God had been that it hadn't carried over into life. Once I saw (though very imperfectly) the meaning of Jesus' words, "A good man gives out good—from the goodness stored in his heart," it was natural to consider every relationship in the light of what I knew of God.

What we are in everyday life shows the kind of thinking we do, far more than the performance of religious duties does. A dear friend is an example of this. She is an influence for Christ on everyone she meets because she is *good*. She's not pious, nor over spiritual in her conversation. She doesn't lead Bible classes nor give testimonies nor take an active part in women's work. She is just the sort of person who is helpful and encouraging in her attitude toward others. That's the sort of goodness Jesus described as "goodness stored in the heart."

This sort of undercurrent to the surface of life is going on all the time. From the time our children are small we are, by our words and tone of voice as well as by our example, having an effect on their growth as human beings. A friend who is a psychologist once said, "If you tell a child he's stupid often enough, he'll be stupid." That's the negative side of the truth that we all are in some way affecting everyone around us, for good or for ill.

The important matter for us each to consider is not so much *my* identity, how I am growing, but the effect I am having on others. One truth to be tucked away and remembered is that one's own identity does better, grows into a more robust plant if it isn't dug up all the time to be scrutinized. A healthy unconcern with self is better than constant introspection. It's less boring for others, too. How heartwarming it is when we talk with someone genuinely interested in life around him and how quickly do we tire of the person who chatters on and on about his affairs, his feelings, his reactions.

It really doesn't matter that, in the beginning, we see imperfectly and understand only fragmentarily; the important thing is to begin acting on what we know to be true. That is, when we see that God loves us even when we are not lovable, even when we are disobedient, rebellious, like pouting children, we must enact that kind of love in our lives. We won't do it too well, of course. Old emotional habits are very strong. But we must begin somewhere. The stamp on our lives we were all meant to have—love for one another like Christ has for us—must begin to make its imprint, or we are merely cardboard Christians, all front and nothing behind.

There is a certain danger in discussing identity and its connection with human relationships. We may oversimplify what is really intricate and complex, reduce that which is ultimately mysterious and indefinable to a tidy but incomplete system. We must remind ourselves that we are, all of us, complicated beings, full of enigmas, ambiguities, and paradoxes. While every one of us is necessarily affected by those around, we are not merely the product of how others regard us. Some traits are so strong they defy every modifying influence. We may misread, or fail to see entirely, the attitudes and reactions of people toward us. And beyond everything, the supreme mystery, is the work God is doing in every human life. We can attempt to see a little more clearly what we are, and how we make or mar each other's lives, but we can never penetrate the depths of the human personality.

Now that my children are grown and married, with children of their own, they sometimes tell me what they thought at certain points in their childhood. I am always amazed at how little I knew, how insensitive I was at the time, and how deeply they were affected by factors I hadn't thought important.

Acknowledging the ultimate mystery each human personality is at bottom does not prevent us, however, from recognizing certain patterns that take place in our lives.

The good, constructive characteristics need to be encouraged while negative tendencies—arrogance, unrestrained temper, self-centeredness, malice, envy—need to be done away with. Since our imperfect human nature makes complete rooting out impossible, we do the next best thing; we try to whittle them down, to shrink them. There are those who believe, sincerely enough, that if one simply prays about such unhappy traits, God will do something about them; one's identity will be brightened by asking earnestly to be delivered from temper or lust or greed.

It hasn't worked that way for me. The Lord has never simply removed an unpleasant habit or tendency, however fervent my prayer. He has, however, provided me with opportunities to choose between various attitudes, or moods, or courses of action. And out of those choices, and because of them, I shape and mold and modify all that goes to make me what I am.

105 / Identity in Relationships

For instance, it was very difficult for me to admit having made a mistake or done something stupid—I was so afraid of being despised for my failures. Honesty is such an integral part of the Christian life, though, that I knew I must begin to be honest. It was one of the hardest things I had ever done, when, for the first time, I called a friend to apologize for a blunder I'd made and successfully covered up. But it was the beginning of a new security for me. Admitting my failures freed me of the fear of failure. As I grew less taut and nervous, I was able to carry out successfully projects I'd never have attempted before. I made lots of mistakes and learned through my blunders. But I was learning that no one accomplishes very much without some false starts and failures, and that it's keeping on that counts, not infallibility.

It has always been fatally easy for us to go at things backward, just as I did in the matter of identity. I thought my identity was the way I happened to feel about myself at the moment. Before I was a Christian I didn't like myself too well most of the time; as a result I had a very bad self-image. But there were other times (not too frequent) when, due to some small triumph, I felt arrogant and self-confident. Then my self-image was very good. In neither case, however, was my mental picture of myself true. Sometimes blurred and distorted by negative feelings, and sometimes blown up to grotesque proportions by momentary elation, what I pictured myself to be was never the reality.

As a young Christian this same subjectiveness might

have continued, giving me a sense of false spirituality and spurious satisfaction, had not God intervened, mercifully enough, by forcing me to look at my relationships with people. I have described this process (highly oversimplified and compressed) and how it led me to a sobering examination of myself and the way in which Jesus Christ was being allowed to work in my life. The humiliating fact was that he wasn't being allowed to work very much, because I had kept him safely penned up in my bedroom, where I had my devotions and said my prayers every morning.

Once I let him out into the rest of my life—into the kitchen and the living room and the streets of Hollywood where I did my shopping and drove to appointments—there was no stopping him. Changes in my attitudes had to be made. There weren't too many alterations in what I *did,* because I'm a coward by nature and much too timid for any flamboyant sinning. But there were severe modifications of attitude. My sins, I saw, were the secret sins of pride, malice, envy, and the like. They don't show up as obviously as the more sensational social sins, but they play havoc with human relationships and they have no place in the true personhood God has designed for us.

The hurt feelings I had cherished (and coddled) when my husband let business appointments interfere with my social plans were the result of pride. I wanted to be first. I had to give up the luxury of wallowing in self-pity because other things sometimes took priority in my husband's life. Being careless about time, which I had always excused on the grounds that I had too much to do was, I came to see, arrogance: I figured my time was more valuable than anyone else's. And so it went—and so it goes. The process of becoming a real person never ends.

It seems to me now that the search for identity can only end successfully when we are really looking for something else. As long as I focused all my thinking on myself—who was I? how would I achieve self-discovery, whatever that was?—I got nowhere. You can't find anything in a vacuum. But when I turned, out of a kind of loneliness and an extremity of despair of myself, to God, I found myself. A very nebulous, undeveloped self, to be sure, but something real. Again, when I turned inward in my naïve efforts to develop a relationship with Christ, I kept bumping into all sorts of frustrating blocks. Only in turning away from self-contemplation to a serious consideration of other people did my own identity begin to take shape.

We mature really only in relationships. God has designed us so that our dependence upon him, as the source and redeemer of life, puts us in position to relate to other people. We are his creation. So are they. We have dignity as human beings. So do they. There would be no way for any of us to develop intellectually, emotionally, or spiritually *all alone*. Relationship and exchange are the means by which we grow up.

11. Identity in Function

I was very fortunate to be a child of the depression. Although I was as worried as today's noisier young people over the problem of my identity, I worried in secret and only in spare moments. Because as soon as school was finished, it was an immediate necessity for me to get a job.

I felt ill-used, I'm sure, but there it was. My parents could not afford to support me while I pondered life's great issues and tried to find out who I was. I knew what I *wasn't* and what I did *not* want to be, but not what I was or could be.

So I got a job, and felt lucky to do so. The streets were full of college graduates looking for work, any work, whether it was in their field or not. There were no representatives of large firms combing the campuses looking for bright young men, no opportunities to weigh the advantages of this position against that one or to inquire into pension plans and vacation and medical allowances. Any job would do.

It was all very demeaning, I thought, having to set my mind on the commonplace, even trivial, matters necessitated by my job instead of bending all efforts toward more momentous matters. And what connection did what I was doing have to who I really was? Years later, all I had felt then swept over me in a flash as I listened to an earnest young undergraduate telling me, "Sometimes I just go off by myself and think deep thoughts!"

Like other discontented young men and women, I too thought deep thoughts. I wondered about my identity —but not for long. There wasn't time. Although I didn't know it, that was a great boon, and would ultimately provide the answers I was looking for.

In fact, it was not until I had been married over twenty years and had children nearly grown up that I realized what had been happening. I had been *growing into* my identity, and the manner of the growing lay in my function in life. Not my job—my function. There had been many jobs—secretary, housekeeper, cook, dishwasher, errand-runner—but only one function. I was the wife and the mother of the family, the friend of my friends, a citizen of the U.S.A. and the world.

I say it was one function because there are no neat divisions between the various roles we all play: wife, mother, friend, citizen, housekeeper, club member, consumer. All these overlap. We all play these various roles, but not as an actor who assumes a part for three hours on the stage and then takes it off with the grease-paint. We live roles proper to our station in life, and each role has its functions.

My role as wife and mother, for instance, requires me to function as a cook part of every day. It's my belief that one ought to be able to do any such job passably well; incompetence, if it's deliberate, is an affront to those who are affected by what we do. It says they're not important enough to merit a job well done. Cooking, however, soon meant more to me than just part of my function in the home. It gave me scope for such creativity as I have, and when the results were good the pleasure my family expressed was reward enough, not to mention that fact that I like to eat well too. Cooking became a means of expressing my own originality, even of showing something of my identity.

Cleaning house, on the other hand, though it shows something of my nature, I'm sure, remains something I do because it needs to be done. It's pretty pedestrian. But both the jobs that are fun and those that are purely routine are a means of demonstrating identity; they tell something about me, and at the same time they help to make that identity clearer and stronger. How do you become an organized person for instance? No one is born with that ability. I'm learning to be well organized and efficient by planning my day's work, by doing tasks as quickly and as well as possible, by writing engagements down and by reconciling my bank account.

I didn't discover this all at once, of course. No blinding light made me aware that one's identity cannot be found apart from one's function. It was a gradual realization that *through* fulfilling my function I had come to know my identity. It was no longer necessary to go through any agonizing soul-searching. I knew I was someone loved by God, who had relationships and responsibilities to other people. I was not Eileen Guder all alone in a void, but the Eileen Guder who stood in a special relationship to my husband, and functioned as his wife; who had an equally unique relationship to each of my children and in that capacity did what no one else could do. In doing what I was called upon to do, I was *becoming* what I most wanted to be—a person in proper relationship to those around me.

That does not imply perfection, of course, or that the relationships were, or are, without rough spots from time to time. There are plenty of flaws, which any acquaintance could no doubt point out. But flaws and rough spots notwithstanding, I had a satisfying sense of being me. For the first time I was thankful for that early economic necessity to work which had kept me from indulging the desire simply to wait around to see if I could find myself. I was equally glad for the demands of the family which meant that I had to get up in the morning whether I felt like it or not, had to cook and clean and sew and *be* a mother.

When I did something I knew to be right and proper for the situation, my knowing it was right moved from the realm of the abstract to the personal. In that sense, you never know what it is to be a mother until you are one, and must do all the things a mother does. Knowing, translated into being, becomes knowing on a

The Naked I / 112

deeper level than the intellectual. Simply thinking profound thoughts would have gotten me nowhere. Thoughts may be the true measure of a person, but unless they are expressed in some kind of living, they aren't really thoughts at all, only wish-dreams which vanish in the daylight.

It seems impossible to me to separate the ideas of relationship and function. By the word "function" I mean one's role in life, whether in business or a profession or not. We all have a function in life, a capacity, province, or sphere. But whatever it is, it exists only in relationship with others.

Out of those relationships we come to know ourselves, to be sure of our own identity. After all, what is it that makes us sure of our uniqueness, or selfhood, except the difference between ourselves and all others. The very thing that divides us as human beings—our individual separateness—is the means by which we come to know one another. I can speak to you because you are other than myself; you listen, and then (hopefully) reply. In this communication we come to know ourselves as well as each other. I don't suppose amoebas (supposing them to have self-consciousness) have any knowledge of self until they separate themselves.

In addition to separateness, there must also be some sort of identification for two people to know each other, usually found in the way they relate to each other. No one teaches us this; we learn by being in a world that is set up that way. I cannot remember when I didn't know that my mother stood in a very special relationship to me. There were other people in my small circle: the elderly housekeeper who lived with us the first few years of my life; my father and younger brothers; close neighbors; aunts and family friends. But my mother was special. I depended upon her, and it was to her that I ran when I was hurt or frightened. There was even a very special kind of authority that was hers, different from my father's authority.

My father was a far sterner, more awe-inspiring figure in my life; mother's authority, while at times to be feared (I never *quite* forgot the peach-tree switches so available to her hand) was tempered with softness. I'm very grateful both for my father's role in life—the ultimate authority in the family, sterner, less yielding than my mother—and for her more flexible kind of authority.

At any rate, most children growing up begin very early in life to understand there are different parts for each member of the family to play, and in each one's particular relationship to the others lies his function— and his identity.

In the very beginning, God first gave Adam and Eve their proper role to play: "Be fruitful and multiply, and replenish the earth, and subdue it: and have dominion over the fish of the sea, and over the fowl of the air, and over every living thing that moveth upon the earth." Man was given responsibilities, and relationships; he stood in authority over the creatures of the earth, and was given work to do.

The idea of self-fulfillment, of self-knowledge, apart from work (or, if you dislike the word, from function) is a self-defeating one. *Nothing* can be known in emptiness. We must put something there, or the emptiness will swallow up everything.

At one period in my marriage I had a very silly idea that Russ ought to love me just as I was, apart from anything I did as a wife and mother. Real love, I thought rebelliously, would make no demands on me. Why should I have to be a good cook, and keep an orderly house, and do all the many jobs mothers of young children do? I felt like a slave. Fortunately I was either too cowardly or too serious about my duties as a mother to test this remarkable theory. I kept right on doing what I was supposed to do. It was a long time before I realized that it was so much a part of me to keep house a certain way, and to cook because I loved to, and to sew for the children, that to stop doing those things would have been to cease being me. The person my husband loved was the Eileen-who-does-things-this-way-and-not-that. My function was part of me.

It may well be that self-knowledge, like happiness, can never be found by looking for it. It will come only as a result of something else, namely fulfilling one's proper role in life. This may change from time to time —from being a son or daughter in the family and under parental authority, to being a student and an adult; a worker, a friend, a father or mother. It is certain that we must all do the thing at hand, whatever it is; we can't demand a different role in life arbitrarily. People do, of course, but it usually doesn't work out too well. The teenager who wants to assume an adult role, the discontented housewife who'd rather be a singer, the husband who longs to be an unencumbered bachelor again—all these discover that the new roles they've decided to assume make their own demands upon personality and ability and integrity.

There is a time, as the writer of Ecclesiastes said, for everything under the sun. Part of wisdom consists of recognizing the time for each performance, each changing responsibility.

Christians often think of themselves as being approved by God primarily on account of their spirituality—how ardently they pray, how long and faithfully they read the Bible, or how zealously they witness. The Bible speaks of man's obligation to God in a much broader sense. It talks quite bluntly about work. Paul, the great apostle of grace, was not afraid to use the word "work": "But any man who builds on the foundation using as his material gold, silver, precious stones, wood, hay or stubble, must know that each man's work will one day be shown for what it is. The day will show it plainly enough, for the day will arise in a blaze of fire, and that fire will prove the nature of each man's work. If the work that the man has built upon the foundation will stand this test, he will be rewarded."

The emphasis on work found all the way through the Bible holds a clue to our search for identity; we learn more about who we are by how we work. That is, work in the broadest sense—our way of doing everything, from reading a book or playing a game or handling a job. Work turns out to be almost a synonym for responsibility—function.

Jesus told the skeptical Jews, "My Father is still at

work and therefore I work as well." Later he said, "The work that the Father gave me to complete, yes, these very actions which I do are my witness that the Father has sent me." In other words, his identity was attested to by what he did—his actions.

In a much lesser sense, but in the same sense, we build our own identity as we accept the role in life we have before us, carry out its responsibilities and functions. Actions—work—do not earn us any merit before God. But they demonstrate who we are, both to ourselves and to the world around us.

12. Filling the Role

*T*he word *"role"* has come to have one unfortunate connotation. It suggests a part in a play, a sort of walk-through behavior, all show and no substance. It also means, according to the dictionary, a part or function taken or assumed by anyone. It is inevitable that we all take on various roles, as we have already seen. But that doesn't mean pretending or hypocrisy in the playing of them. That may occur, of course, but the fault is with the intent of the person, not with the fact that life doles out parts for everyone.

The substance of a role is not appearance but function, and this is where we get down to the hard core of life. Function implies work and work is not always looked upon with favor. A great many of our technical advances have been made in the name of doing away with work. And if we can get rid of work, it must be bad, like cancer, polio, and the aging process.

Now this insidious depicting of work as a thing to be conquered, like disease, is the sell of the century, a gigantic hoax bought by too many gullible souls. How could we have been so foolish? From the time we made mud-pies, imitating the work our mothers did in the kitchen, children have been bored by too much play.

"What can I do now, mother?" has been the plaintive question of children surrounded by toys and amusements whose ingenuity and variety are bewildering in their plenitude. Simply offering another form of amusement won't answer.

It doesn't matter what you call it, too much playing is deadly. Leisure, as opposed to work, is simply the same old endless stretch of empty hours. It only becomes alive and has meaning when it is used for work —not labor which earns a living, but work of some kind. Then leisure is constructive. It allows time to do other work than that which brings in the paycheck. Whatever one uses such leisure for—studying, painting, stamp collecting, folk dancing, taking classes— it's not play, but *different* work. That's why it's good.

I used to watch my children playing, and much of the time they were pretending to work. They didn't arrange the blocks into meaningless shapes, or the building logs into just any pattern. They made buildings. My little girls drew stick figures with out-of-round heads which they solemnly called "mommies," and they were shown sweeping, making pies, spanking their children, but never just sitting. And there was a truth there. To be a mother means doing certain things; it involves function.

Being a mother may necessitate taking care of a home, washing and ironing and minding children; or it may mean, as it does for many young wives helping their husbands through school, dropping the baby off at the baby-sitters', working at a desk all day and then coming home to dinner and a few jobs before fatigue pulls one into bed. In either case, there is work involved. The function is part of the role.

While it is true that identity lies not in the role one plays, but in relationship to God who reveals to us who we are, the way we fill out the role reveals our identity. How we function tells who we are. I have found that in attempting to describe someone in the sense of making them known, there are normally two facts about them that I mention. The first is what the person does. That fact may not convey anything at all definitive, it may even be misleading; yet we all have, in our thinking, invested occupations with characteristics of their own.

To say, "He is a judge," carries with it all sorts of images—courtrooms, the severity and intricacies of law, dignity (perhaps even pomposity), to begin with. Each of us adds his own concepts to the image. "Judge" brings to me the picture of shelves of legal textbooks and reference works—very heavy, somewhat dusty. I also see a remote figure either entering or leaving the courtroom. That is probably because my experience of jury duty left me with a predominant impression of brief court sessions interspersed with frequent—and lengthy—adjournments.

On the other hand, when someone tells me, "Oh,

she's an artist," my mind immediately flashes before me several images: a figure in a paint-streaked cover-all; stacks of canvases around an untidy room; the figure painting furiously, ignoring doorbells and ringing phones. Now this may be a wildly inaccurate picture of the particular artist being described to me, but that's the first impression the word conveys to me.

We all realize that such impressions, while inevitable, are not very accurate, so descriptions seldom stop there. The second item in describing someone we know is nearly always based on how that person affects us. And nine times out of ten, the way he or she functions will be part of the general feeling we have. Like this:

"She's one of the sweetest women I've ever known; but not a bit saccharine or sentimental. I'd trust her with my deepest secrets because she never gossips. We've been friends for years, closer than sisters, really." (A good friend, discreet, who welcomes confidences and is able to give friendship beyond the surface level.)

"Oh, him? Great guy, marvelous storyteller. He certainly livens up a dinner party, but don't ask him to serve on a committee—all talk and no action—you know the kind." (Pleasant enough, but the speaker has been let down a couple of times and is a bit irritated with good old Joe.)

"He's a good worker—always dependable. He'll do a good job. But I don't think I'd ask him to be chairman. He's—well, he's a nice guy, but . . ." (The speaker thinks he's pretty dull.)

"Why on earth did they invite *her*? We'll never get it off the ground, she doesn't know the meaning of time. You watch, she'll sail in an hour late and think a charming apology makes it all right. *I* could have told them she'd never do, she means well but just can't manage." (She is likable but slops through life, annoying everyone including the person speaking.)

The way we behave does show something of our identity, not our spiritual standing before God, which depends on his grace, but our performance. As Christians we make that distinction, aware of the biblical command not to judge each other. However, the New Testament also lays great stress on being patient with each other, putting up with one another's weaknesses, and being forgiving. Such spiritual exercises (for they are that) are only called for by obvious faults in us all, and when you're constantly having to overlook someone's irritating habits you are very much aware of them. Being aware of them means thinking something about the person—a value judgment if you like.

When my friends forgive my lapses into unpunctuality and say, "Eileen's late again—she tried to do too many jobs this morning and just phoned to say she's on her way," they may be kind and Christian but they're also observant. They see something of my unrealistic approach to the limits of time; I'm always trying to squeeze more into an hour than it will hold. That's me, part of my identity, and since it's a flaw, I'm trying to get rid of it. As I improve in my handling of the work I have to do and my allocation of time, that shows something of my identity too. It says that I'm aware of my fault in this regard and am willing to change.

Everyone of us constantly shows something of our identity, then, by the way we function in life. It may not be the true person whom only God knows, but it's all there is of us for those around us to know. The Sermon on the Mount is all about how behavior and attitudes show what we are. The people who belong to the kingdom of God will live a certain way and you will recognize them by their fruits. We're not perfect, certainly—not finished products—but people in the process of becoming what God intends us to be.

John, no doubt thinking of our unfinished quality as children of God, said, "We don't know what we shall become in the future. We only know that, if reality were too break through, we should reflect his likeness, for we should see him as he really is!"

All true. Not only do we have a very dim apprehension of Jesus, but we cannot see ourselves clearly, nor anyone else. Our knowledge is incomplete. We ought not to judge the spiritual standing of anyone, since we never have all the facts. Acceptance of one another's weaknesses is essential to the Christian life—or, really, to any kind of harmonious life, Christian or otherwise, but especially commanded by Jesus of his followers.

Nevertheless, we cannot live a single day without making value judgments. *This is good, that is lacking in value, I ought not to have done it, she spoke very unkindly, his conduct makes me wonder about his honesty.* These thoughts are natural and suitable for moral, thinking human beings. They are part of the necessity to choose which has been with us since the snake offered Eve the first fruit. We are constantly deciding among a bewildering abundance of possibilities. We must make value judgments, or the words "good" and "evil" and their mixture of which life consists are without meaning.

It is this inevitable human evaluation of people and situations to which Jesus was referring when he said that a bad tree produces bad fruit just as a good tree brings good fruit. You know a man, like a tree, by the fruit it bears. Underlying the Sermon on the Mount is the principle that what is in a man's heart (his identity) will assuredly be shown in his life. Everyone knew what he meant when he referred to the Pharisees' showy piety as hypocrisy. They put up a marvelous façade of spirituality but the barrenness of their religiosity was plain to see.

"Good works" in the biblical sense means more than the performance of certain pious or civic-minded duties. It is the manner in which they are done, their *style* which stamps them either genuine or only imitation piety. To use a present-day illustration, it's the difference between a woman who snarls at her husband and children in private, whose temper and impatience make home miserable, but who presents a public façade of patience and sweetness, and the woman whose treatment of her family is the same whether alone or in company. Or the secretary who slops through her work, cadging help from the other girls in the office, always blaming someone else for a lost file, all the while managing to appear brisk and busy when the boss is around, as contrasted with the woman who does her day's work as efficiently as she knows how. They may both look the same to the casual visitor passing through the office, but only one is genuine.

It is the genuineness of our performance which is always under scrutiny, since how we work tells so much about who we are. There are many roles in life, many roles in each life. Each one has its proper responsibilities and obligations. The style with which we carry them out tells more than our ability for that particular job, it displays something of our real identity. Kind or careless, transparent or devious, sensitive or coarse, timid or arrogant—or the strange mixture of contradictions most of us are—all these shade every role we fill.

We are more than the roles we play. But the way we carry them out, what we do, shows what we are.

13. The Limits
of the Role

A very dear friend in Washington, D. C., is a minister's wife. It is a role she is called upon to play in her relationship with the members of her husband's church. At home, however, she is the one who pulls food out of the refrigerator at odd times to suit her family's erratic schedule, runs errands, keeps the house running smoothly, and always listens to whatever problems and/ or confidences her family bring her, at whatever time they want to talk—however inconvenient it is for her. As a friend she is noted for arranging things so everyone will be comfortable; for working out sightseeing schedules at a moment's notice when people arrive panting to "really *see* Washington," and often ending up as baby-sitter for her guests. She slips in and out of her many roles during the day with astonishing ease —because she is sure of her identity.

Another acquaintance plays only one role, whatever

the relationship—boss. At home, on a committee, at lunch with other women, or having her hair done, she tells everyone what to do and how to do it. She only knows one way to be in a relationship—dominant. I sometimes think she's doing what we are all prone to —confusing her identity with her various roles. In order to be sure of herself she must always enact the same part. How do we avoid confusing the two, identity and role?

The many relationships in my life have each demanded a different role of me. As a child, my role was to be subordinate to my parents, to learn, to submit to discipline, and to respond to their love. With my friends, my roles involved being submissive to some, dominating with others, and meeting still others as an equal. Each role demonstrates my identity.

At the same time, whether I like it or not or am satisfied with it or not, my identity, what I am, acts on others and evokes from them a definite response. One of the purposes of Christ's work in us is to develop each one of us in our relationship to him that our reactions to each other will be transformed. Instead of responding on an instinctive, purely human level, our identity as people who belong to Christ modifies all our reactions so that we act *out of a knowledge of who we are* rather than on the basis of what has been done or said to us.

We have been taught to do this in other areas and on other levels than the Christian ethic. Christ simply raised what is already known and practiced to its ultimate and true meaning. Little boys are taught not to hit girls because "boys *do not* hit girls!" The idea is implanted that there are certain ways boys behave, and certain other acts just not compatible with being a boy. Some of these ideas may be silly, of course—like the one that boys don't cry, which must be a fairly recent idea, because up until a century or two ago men wept freely and without shame.

All our lives we have been learning certain ways of living and acting on the basis of who we are. It would seem that a strong sense of identity ought to be naturally developed by this emphasis. That this is not the case we have already seen, and for very good reason; we are always appealed to on the basis of a certain role in life—son or daughter, student, employee—not on the basis of our real selves. Identity and role have been confused.

When I was a little girl I often felt very rebellious about the tight discipline my parents enforced. Would they still love me if I didn't conform to their standards of behavior? I felt somehow that real love ought to be given, even when I was naughty. I know now that my father and mother did love me when I was naughty, but their displeasure was so terrible when I disobeyed that I was sure the love was gone.

That is the common experience of children growing up. All of us who have been parents are horrified when we discover that we, in turn, have helped our children to confuse their identity with their role and have failed to assure them of unfailing, constant love. That's why it is so difficult for most of us to understand that God loves us just as we are. Once we grasp the idea that his love never changes (that his wrath against sin is the other side of his love), we are on our way to becoming real persons.

I see quite clearly now that my parents, without in the least intending to, constantly conveyed the idea that I had to behave a certain way because I was a little girl, or only a child—in short, because of a role which I knew would be temporary. I could hardly wait to grow up, so as to get rid of all these restrictions. My role was mixed up with my identity.

The confusion may be inevitable, but it goes when we find ourselves at last in relationship to Christ. Then we are freed to begin taking our various roles, not out of a sense of compulsion or obligation, but freely because we are secure in ourselves. I *had* to find my identity in order to satisfactorily fulfill my various roles.

Paul was talking about roles when he wrote,

Children, the right thing for you to do is to obey your parents as those whom the Lord has set over you. . . . Fathers, don't overcorrect your children or make it difficult for them to obey the commandment. . . . Slaves, obey your human masters sincerely with a proper sense of respect and responsibility, as service rendered to Christ himself. . . . And as for you employers, be as conscientious and responsible towards those who serve you as you expect them to be toward you. . . .

This description of our various roles comes near the end of the letter to the Ephesians, which begins by telling us who we are:

Praise be to the God and Father of our Lord Jesus Christ for giving us through Christ every possible spiritual benefit as citizens of Heaven! For consider what he has done—before the foundation of the world he chose us to become, in Christ, his holy and blameless children living within his constant care. He planned, in his purpose of love, that we should be adopted as his own children through Jesus Christ—that we might learn to praise the glorious generosity of his which has made us welcome in the everlasting love he bears toward the Beloved.

We are, then, citizens of heaven, children of God beloved by him. That is our identity. I am a *specific* child of God, just as you are. Since the Bible is full of statements about his love, concern, and interest in each one of us, and the world around demonstrates his infinite creativity and variety, I know that the unique, this-and-not-thatness that is *me* is his design.

The constant reminders in the New Testament about the proper way to live our various roles are always based on who we are—children of God. Perhaps no one except the Christian can really be heart-whole in any role, because only the Christian's identity will not be destroyed by time. We know that in putting ourselves in the hands of Christ we have stepped from time to eternity, and our "home base" is beyond this world.

Again and again Paul wrote about the identity Christians have—and how it ought to be displayed in the various roles we play. Writing to the Colossians, he reminded them they were no longer strangers to God, but reconciled through Christ's death . . . that Christ was in them . . . that they shared a new life . . . that they were "risen" with Christ . . . that they were God's "picked representatives" of the new humanity. Their identity was to be shown, he went on, as they were "merciful in action, kindly in heart, humble in mind." *Then* he continued to give some specific instructions on the way this would work out in various roles, just as he did to the people at Ephesus. Wives, children, husbands, employees, bosses—each had certain responsibilities proper to his station in life.

The phrase "station in life" may have an old-fashioned sound, but it conveys the truth about the way things are. We do have various stations in life, which is another way of saying we have different roles in life. Much of the confusion (and silliness) today is because so many people cannot accept the fact that they have a role to play. They want to be everything—and so they are nothing.

Wives and mothers try to look and act as if they were twenty and single. Middle-aged men adopt the manners and appearance of youthful playboys. Students in college would rather reorganize society than be students. And among a certain group of the young, the boys and girls look so much alike that one can only conclude they don't care for the sex they were born with.

This is all wishful thinking. No one can play every role without failing to fulfill the demands of any role at all. It's no narrow, restrictive limit on life to say, "I am this and not that. I can do some things, but not all things." Particularity is the only way to express who we are. It follows, of course, that we are given certain roles to play, and the best thing to do is to fulfill the demands of the present roles as well as we can.

That means giving wholehearted attention to the duties of the present hour. It's no use wishing one had some other role in life. The time may come, as it did for me, when the role changes abruptly.

For years the primary roles I lived were those of wife and mother, and my functions in life had to do with running a house, raising children, buying, planning, cleaning, entertaining. Then my husband died, both my children left home and married, and my roles changed. I was writing books and speaking to church groups. Different roles—same identity. I missed having young people around as they had been when my children were home, and I missed the entertaining I had done—the barbecues in the patio, potluck dinners, and the fun of feeding hungry young men and women who made me feel like a gourmet cook.

There were new experiences, though, which called for different capabilities than those I had used in my home. I traveled more, met new people and learned that being a speaker at luncheons and dinners demanded other abilities from me than those of wife and mother. It also brought different rewards.

As a result, my advice to all is, enjoy what you are called to do now, as all things pass away and the responsibilities *and pleasures* of the present, once gone, can never return. Every role has not only its proper duties, functions, and obligations, but also its own felicity. Enjoyment of the pleasure proper to a role goes with acceptance of its obligations. You cannot have one without the other, though the world is full of people trying to enjoy the rewards of several roles while avoiding the obligations of any of them.

The end result of trying to separate pleasure from obligation is a profound dissatisfaction with oneself, and with the diversions so anxiously pursued, and a bored, aimless existence accompanied by a nagging sense of nonidentity. These people are the "lost" whom Jesus came to save. He offers not only true identity but calls us to our proper roles within that identity.

14. God's Originals

A young minister on the staff of a large church remarked recently that it was amazing to discover how many people felt that all Christians ought to think alike on everything. He frequently received phone calls from distressed and/or righteously indignant church members who had unearthed a dreadful heresy: nonconformity. The refrain was always the same.

"How can a member of *our* church," they would cry, "be in favor of sex education in the schools?" Or vote the Democratic ticket (Republicanism being apparently the hallmark of a Christian) or prefer modern translations of the Bible to the sacred King James, or believe in ecumenism, or go to cocktail parties, or enjoy folk rock music, or gaze unmoved and unalarmed at hordes of long-haired youth coming to evening church, or read Tillich, or take a positive attitude toward the phrase "social action."

All of us will react—have already reacted—to each of these subjects. We either like or dislike the idea conveyed by the word or phrase, and being but very imperfect human beings we invariably invest our particular point of view with divine sanction. Angels would know better. I think like this all the time, and so do you. The business of reminding myself that I am *not* all wise or omnipotent and hence might just possibly be mistaken in some of my cherished opinions is a process I go through again and again. It is inevitably painful. I don't enjoy admitting my lack of wisdom nor my proneness to error.

One cannot become a Christian at all, however, without admitting failure and sin and helplessness. Turning to Christ is an admission of one's own inability to go it alone. We all know—or at least we say we know—that becoming Christian does not automatically correct all our deviations nor establish us instantly as perfected people. We talk about the need for God's forgiveness and about growing in grace. Why is it then that so often we behave as if we were already perfect, already know everything, and immediately consign to outer darkness all those who disagree with our views of life? Why do we assume that the really spiritual person will agree with my politics, my tastes in music and art and church government, and even my theology?

The relationships which we find in the Bible are usually relationships of people who are different from each other, whose unity lay in their faith in Christ not in their being alike. Peter, James, John, Andrew, and

Philip emerge from the pages of Scripture with quite definite personalities and varying attitudes toward their situation. Paul's letters are full of practical advice on getting along together with Christians of different persuasions about Christian behavior. Everything from meat-eating versus vegetarianism to which holy days ought to be observed came under his scrutiny. In every case his conclusion was, "Don't judge —don't criticize—be patient with each other—cultivate forbearance."

These discussions on Christian differences always are linked, in Paul's letters, with good advice on relationships. There's a very good reason for this— we cannot consider getting along with each other without taking into account our differences. There is no hint in the Bible that we ought to erase all distinguishing marks and fit ourselves into identical molds. That is the way the world thinks, and Paul's opinion of conformity is shown in his admonition to the Christians in Rome: "Don't let the world around you squeeze you into its own mold, but let God remold your minds from within . . . ." He followed that sentence with some fatherly counsel about not getting exaggerated ideas of one's own importance and about carrying out whatever duties one has ability to do in a worthy manner. No hint of conformity here.

A little later on he advised the same people not to become too set in their own opinions. Paul was a realist, and in every letter he wrote he included a caution about arrogance (*I* am always right) and exhortations, sometimes quite lengthy, to respect one another's differences. "Do look at things which stare you in the face!" he wrote. "So-and-so considers himself to belong to Christ. All right; but let him reflect that we belong to Christ every bit as much as he."

The very word "relationship" carries with it the implication of otherness. It is the connection between one person and objects or persons around him, things other than himself. Otherness implies difference, and difference implies variety. That's what makes this a fascinating world. We like variety and find that lack of it brings boredom; but at the same time we are afraid of it. This fear, I believe, comes from our own inner uncertainty. When we aren't sure of our own beliefs we are very sensitive, very defensive about them. They mustn't be touched in any way lest they crumble and leave us without anything. Hence, people who state opinions that contradict ours or behave in a way strange to us are threatening. If they are right, we must be wrong and that would be intolerable.

For a person tied up in this kind of box, every single relationship is a tenuous and fragile connection. When opinions and attitudes are similar enough, the timid soul, so frightened lest his tidy little box of beliefs be disturbed, can relax and accept the one whose box is just like his own. But when he meets those who think differently than he does, whose opinions don't match his own, he becomes antagonistic, even aggressive. The rigid thinkers who seem so overbearing, who are so militant in eradicating deviations from their particular viewpoint, are really a quivering mass of fear. The arrogance and apparent strength are only surface, and have their origin in an inner anxiety which must banish anything that might crack the brittle structure of opinion. Opinion is the proper word to use—or perhaps prejudice, or bias—because "faith" would not suit at all. Faith *is* trust in what one believes, and is much too durable to be shattered by rubbing against different beliefs.

People who are sure enough of their own position to be untroubled by different points of view can sustain good strong relationships with those of very different opinions. It doesn't mean they're right, or even that they won't change. It simply means they have a healthy conviction in their *essential rightness* based on trust in Jesus Christ, so they can accept the possibility that much of their thinking may be incomplete, or in error. Their security lies not in their ideas but in their Savior, and because their safety lies in Jesus and not in themselves and their own thinking, they can be open to those who think differently than they do.

It seems to me that much of the tension, schism, and strained suspicion in much of the Christian world stems from a deep inner uncertainty, which can produce only poor relationships. The church ought to be the one place where all Christians can find acceptance. It ought to be the one body of people so related to one another in openness and love that we are evidence to the world that Jesus Christ transforms people. That's what he meant his church to be.

When this does happen—when groups of people live like this—something wonderful happens. Not only does the quality of love and friendship serve as an effective witness to the world, but we begin to appreciate the shadings and colorations of the rich variety of human nature. We can permit people to be themselves instead of trying to fit them into a mold of our own shaping. God never meant life to be boring, but his people often make it that way. Worse, we make God a bore by insisting that everyone he touches be exactly as we are.

When God has a free hand, he turns out only originals—no two alike. That means that every relationship will be unique, built out of the personhood of people free to be what they are.

We must keep reminding ourselves that with such diversity of races, cultures, physical and emotional heritages and individualities it would be unreasonable to expect that all this would lead to identical conclusions in thinking. We *do* have unity when it comes to the ultimate questions of life, and that is really all God requires of us. No doubt as Paul traveled from country to country, city to city, each with its own culture, he reflected on the marvelous diversity one finds in the world. His advice to the Christians of those cities and towns, many of which are now nothing but desolate ruins, is as relevant to us today as it was then simply *because* Paul talked about relationships. The qualities and attitudes that made for good relationships then have not changed. Then as now they began with a sound respect for the uniqueness of every human being and acceptance of the differences between us.

Living in the Christian community ought to prepare

us for some of the surprises we shall find in heaven. Our settled notions are always being overturned. Those whom we've categorized and forgotten pop out every now and then with some astonishing departure from what we expected of them. We can never be sure we have everything properly arranged because life is people, and people just won't stay put. All this is good. God is trying to tell us something—that he has not exhausted his creativity and that he hasn't yet shown us all his secrets.

"Things which eye saw not, and ear heard not," wrote Paul, quoting the Old Testament, "and which entered not into the heart of man, whatsoever things God prepared for them that love him." We can't even imagine the richness and variety of God's creativity. The multiplicity of objects and creatures this world is peopled with is nothing, I am sure, compared to the rest of God's creation. We've seen only a small part of his handiwork. We're going to be delighted and astonished when the whole is revealed.

In the meantime, a healthy appreciation of the differences God put into his creatures is proper. After all, I rejoice in being me, and flatter myself (as we all do) that there is no one else in the world exactly like me. There isn't anyone exactly like you, either. Let us each permit God to be original in his work with us. The more sure I am of my identity in Christ, the more I give myself to each role and function in life, the quicker I am to appreciate what he is doing in the lives of others.

Christ at work in the world, in his people, adds

flavor which is unmistakably *his*—but it's not all vanilla.

For further reading—

DELIVER US FROM FEAR. By Eileen Guder. About that many-headed monster, fear: the fear of becoming involved; the fear of change; the fear of rejection; the fear of failure; the fear of death. The author suggests biblical, practical ways of looking our fears in the face, of calling them by name, describing what they do to us, and putting the spiritual remedy—faith—to work. #80415 (hardback).

THE MANY FACES OF FRIENDSHIP. By Eileen Guder. Discovering the characteristics of a good friend . . . one who acts out the kind of service that Jesus asked his friends to give . . . one who is there when the going gets rough . . . one whose presence smooths over the bumps and softens the hurt. #80139 (hardback); #98071 (quality paperback).

RELEASE FROM FEAR AND ANXIETY. By Cecil G. Osborne. Identifies fears and anxieties that plague everyone—the future, other people, failure, guilt, sex, anger. Suggests means and methods for securing your own liberation from self-defeat and for turning anxiety and fear into the benevolent gifts intended by the Creator. #80429 (hardback); #98050 (quality paperback).

PEACE WITH THE RESTLESS ME. By Janice Hearn. A real-life pilgrimage from futility to fulfillment; for Christians who want help in overcoming depression and bitterness in their lives. Baring her soul, Janice Hearn describes the fork in the road of her life and shares what she is learning of how the Holy Spirit transforms the believer's attitudes by working from the inside out. #80455 (hardback).

YES IS A WORLD. By James W. Angell. A rousing welcome into the life of affirmation. This hope-filled book includes chapters titled: Man Is Born With Rainbows in His Heart; Not the Postponed Life; Transcendence Is a Kiss on the Nose; Instructions for Erecting a Tent in a Rainstorm; Yes Got Up Before the Sun; Dancing on a Battlefield. #80387 (hardback).

LOCKED IN A ROOM WITH OPEN DOORS. Ernest T. Campbell. Understanding and wise counsel in the face of: rejection, in all its varied forms; the immobilization that comes from inner struggles, weaknesses, and a whole catalog of fears; sin; man's craving for clarity. #80351 (hardback); #98082 (quality paperback).

SHAPING YOUR FAITH. By C. W. Christian. A guidebook which explains what theology is, why it is essential to faith, and how it grows and develops out of the believer and the church. Answers such questions as where theology comes from, how to understand the questions it raises, how to "do" theology. #80300 (hardback); #98002 (quality paperback).

DARE TO BE YOU. By James R. Dolby. A springboard for fresh thinking and lively discussion in the various areas of your religious experience and daily living. A section "As the Twig Is Bent" traces the emotional and spiritual growth of the child from birth through the college years. #91005 (Key-Word paperback).

BAREFOOT DAYS OF THE SOUL. By Maxie D. Dunnam. A "thank you celebration" for what Christ has done and is doing. How to gain freedom from the strain of self-effort; break out of the box of beliefs you learned by rote; claim the gift of personal wholeness; become an intimate friend of God; enjoy steady, constant growth in your personal relationships. #80432 (hardback).

ALL YOU LONELY PEOPLE/ALL YOU LOVELY PEOPLE. By John Killinger. How often do you admit your loneliness or find escape from its crippling frustration? The author recalls meetings, incidents, confrontations and emotions to demonstrate how people can share each other's lives. Perceptive insights into the very essence of caring relationships. #80315 (hardback).

THE GIFT OF WHOLENESS. By Hal L. Edwards. The warmly human story of a modern pilgrim in search of himself ... and in search of God. A refreshing look at one minister and his ministry—a vulnerable, open kind of life that grows and keeps on growing. #80377 (hardback).

TO KISS THE JOY. By Robert A. Raines. Reveals the author's deep awareness of the painfulness of growth; the yearning for the comfort of yesterday; the sense of fear when faith is threatened. Urges the reader to live boldly, immediately; to live in unison with his dreams, daring to risk much. #80324 (hardback).

THE ONE AND ONLY YOU. By Bruce Larson. A book about you and your uniqueness; about God and the liberating nature of his love for you. Insights for using the past for growth; living in the present with openness, joy, and expectancy; claiming your future; enjoying your strengths; claiming the gift of hope and giving hope away. #80347 (hardback); #91012 (Key-Word paperback).

THE BECOMERS. By Keith Miller. Helpful insights into exploring what conversion really is and how it happens; learning how to penetrate beyond people's defensive filters

to co_____ _____ ____ _____ and _____ e_____lishing
mean_____ _____ _ ____ _____ _____ _____ing all
you v_____n even-
ing w___ ____ ____ _____ _____ ____ ___ (hardback)

THE _____ _____ __ _____ __ _____. A compel-
ling _____ __ ___ Christian faith, _____ _____ __th modern p_____ _____ ___ _____dealism
and v_____ ___ _____ _____ _____ _____ of existence ___ _____ ____ __ ___ _____ _____ s to re-
captu_____world's
indep_____ _____ __ ____ _____ #80342

thirty-
ruggles
ones to
e Phil-
essages.

ow by
tional
self in
ot be

TH. By
er the
r job
; over-
lepres-
vering
back);
C-0627